The Author

Seamus McRory was born in the parish of Lissan in South Derry in Northern Ireland. He was a founder member of the SDLP, becoming chairman of its Falls Branch in West Belfast. When he took up a teaching position in County Longford, in the mid 70's, he left active politics. A former chairman of his native club, with whom he played football in the 1960's and 1970's, he currently represents his adopted club, Longford Slashers, on the Longford County GAA Board.

For the past thirty years, Seamus, a retired Primary school Principal, has contributed many articles and poems to various publications.
He is also the published author of *"The Voice from the Sideline: Famous GAA Managers."* (1997), *"The Road to Croke Park: Great GAA Personalities"* (1999), *"The All-Ireland Dream"(2005)* and *"James McCartan, The King of Down Football."*(2010).

Educated at his local primary school and St Patrick's College, Armagh, Seamus continued his education at St Joseph's College of Education and Queen's University, Belfast. He lives in Abbeycartron, just outside Longford Town, with his wife, Olive and family, Mairéad and Diarmuid.

Dedication

To Olive, Mairéad and Diarmuid for their constant
help and support over the years.

Contents

D - A SPORTING LIFE:
Gaelic Games, Soccer, and Rugby.

E - PERSONAL FAVOURITES:
People who made a difference.
Spiritual Reflections.

Foreword

Over one hundred years ago the Irish Literary Revival, which concentrated on the social, political and romantic happenings of the time, began to assert itself throughout Ireland. During this period the country was experiencing constant change which eventually led to the brilliantly, creative works of Yeats, Lady Gregory, our late distinguished Nobel Prize-winner and Poet Laureate Seamus Heaney, and many more celebrated writers. Now Seamus McRory's new collection of experiences, observations and reflections is another testament to the outstanding contribution of great writers in this country.

Seamus's anthology connects with real people's values and emotions in times both past and present. He identifies with people by writing about nostalgic, childhood memories that we all know and to which we can readily relate as well as recalling moments that we will always treasure and events in our lives that we will continue to appreciate. Each of the five sections depicts contrasting stages and a separate set of memories in his life. In this, his latest work, he reaches unique heights of expression by offering vivid descriptions of what was witnessed, the types of emotions experienced and the various outcomes of events. Seamus's poetic ability creates an avenue for the reader to enjoy, reminisce, and be in awe of such an excellent writer that we have now in our midst.

From the first section - The Formative Years - the happier observations of childhood and rural life in his native Lissan are described in detail and give a deep sense of what it was like to witness a new agricultural machine - The Pick-up Baler.

We stood at the corner of the hayfield
And watched in joyful expectation,
As we observed for the first time,
A new mechanical creation.

As we move through the collection from the days of his youth until the present, the author encounters different challenges, some happy, some sad. This anthology carries a particularly emotional and stark account of events in Northern Ireland, especially during the last thirty years of the twentieth century. His Bloody Sunday Trilogy and his recall of the many tragic events in post - internment Belfast and elsewhere clearly reminds us of a period collectively known as The Troubles, gladly no longer with us. It is in the "Voices of the Victims" that Seamus leaves us in no doubt as to whom he thinks should be remembered most.

Their needs, their feelings should always take precedence,
Over any political or social expediency,
To accommodate those who perpetrated such heinous crimes.
They have been our real patriots, our real heroes who suffered and died
So that the rest of us could find true peace, true freedom.

After dealing comprehensively with the immense suffering that so many people endured in so many ways, Seamus devotes the last two parts of his work to the more enjoyable themes of sport and to people and places that contributed positively to his enjoyment of life in his adopted County of Longford.

He displays a natural interest in all sport and gives very incisive accounts of some of the sporting greats from Christy Ring to a plethora of soccer and rugby stars like Harry Gregg, Bobby Moore, Brian O'Driscoll and Ronan O'Gara. The tremendous skill levels of all these superb athletes on the pitch are accurately replicated and precisely recorded. For me his descriptive profile of Colm "The Gooch" Cooper takes pride of place.

Deft of foot and sleight of hand
He glides effortlessly across Gaelic football's many green pastures.
As if defenders did not exist, as if out for a casual morning stroll.

This anthology is rich in content and all embracing in its variation. It contains realistic and meaningful themes that many a person can enjoy and be captivated with. It is a thoroughly enjoyable and totally unforgettable book.

Sean Kelly MEP.
President of the GAA (2003-2006).

Section A

THE FORMATIVE YEARS:
Rural Life in Lissan.
Boarding School in Armagh.

(1)   The Bluebells Of Lissan Wood

Four centuries ago, the English government colonised a
substantial part of my native parish.
Hundreds of acres of rich, rolling pastureland were confiscated.
And then in the midst of this rural expanse
The magnificent, stately Lissan House was built.
A great hall, a splendid ballroom formed the centrepiece of the
interior.
Outside, purpose-built stables, a large, imposing, walled garden
dominated.
A huge forest of deciduous trees, of every species, flanked the
winding avenue walls.
Our farm bordered this wooden wonderland of rare fauna,
exclusive flora.
In the innocence of my youthful curiosity
I could not understand why this estate was so large, so varied
and all the neighbouring farms so small, so ordinary.

About a hundred yards into the wood, a secluded spring well
neatly nestled
Beneath an ornate arboretum of glossy green-leafed shrubs.
Every week, during my childhood, our whole family went there
to get drinking water.
At the well's edge my father knelt down to lift the heavy, iron lid
from the top of the well,
Before plunging each of our empty containers into the gushing,
noisily flowing water, two feet below.
Filled with the joys of family closeness, we would happily return
home to sample the appetisingly, cool liquid.

We loved those trips, especially in April and May,
When the whole forest floor would be totally covered with a
mass of lavender-blue bluebells,
Whose green, narrow stems, about eight inches high,
Were topped with powerfully scented drooping heads of blue.

If there was a gentle breeze blowing through the trees,
If the melodic chimes of the clock on the tower of Lissan House
were ringing on the hour,
One experienced the most fulfilling feeling of total
enchantment, of aesthetic beauty.
To see thousands of bluebells, in five acres of assembled
happiness,
Nodding their heads in the one direction
With their collective scent, wafting like a sea mist across the
perfumed air,
Was a joyful reminder of the mystery of God's creation.
When the canopy cover closed in above the treetops, the flowers
below disappeared for another year.
Nature was, as always, preparing us for the next seasonal
change,
Its next manifestation of the wonder of life.

One day big Paddy McNally came with a perfectly crafted,
forked stick in his hand.
He ambled out into the front field, observed its linear contours
Before following their undulating pathways.
He tightly clasped each fist around a matching wing of the
divining rod, its short, slender trunk facing horizontally, and
outwards.

He walked slowly forwards, his face intense, and his expression neutral.

Suddenly, but surely, the rod started to turn upwards, inwards and Paddy began to smile.

When it had moved a full ninety degrees, he stopped

And uttered these life-changing words to my father:

"Dominic, there is a very strong spring just below where my feet are.

You will only have to dig about six feet".

Three months later, I returned home for my first break from boarding school.

My father proudly showed me where he had dug a new well, lined it with circular concrete liners.

And then built a galvanised roofed pump house above it.

He told me there was enough water to supply the whole townland.

I had mixed feelings; our days of journeying to the wood were over.

There would be no more shared thoughts of the joys of bluebells in the springtime.

Today, even though a hundred miles away and two generations apart,

I still hanker after those gently, dozing, most agreeable bluebells keeping time to a chiming clock.

Even yet, in my moments of darkness, in my times of excitement,

I promise myself to return some year soon to visit that wonderful world of scented woodland.

(2) The Potato Pit

Having checked all the traps to ensure
That no vermin had penetrated the dormant crop,
Stored in two dozen pits in the potato field behind the dwelling
house,
My father carefully removed the dense, compacted
Layer of dark brown soil on one of them,
To reveal a thick, undercoat of smooth, compressed rushes.
Each covering had helped to preserve the pits of precious
potatoes
From the ravages of winter frost, of excessive dampness.

Around the perimeter of each ran a shallow rainwater trench.
Now the soil was returned there from whence it came
After the digging was completed during the previous autumn.
A large, dark, musty, rectangular woollen blanket
With long, wooden poles at either extremity,
Erected at the northern end,
Served as a protective windshield
From the bitter cold, piercing wind of a March Spring day.

Two cloth kneelers, replete with padded straw,
Were placed at the southern end,
As the rushes were meticulously stripped
To unveil a perfectly solid pyramid of
Mostly uniformly shaped, blue Arran Victory potatoes.
With an open, wire-mesh basket wedged between them,
My mother and father knelt down and worked feverishly
To maximise the limited availability of daily sunlight.

Extra small or too large tubers
Were extracted from the rest
And placed in a separate wooden container.
Each regular potato was firmly clutched in the left hand
And using the forefinger of the right as a lever,
A quick, sharp movement by the adjacent thumb, away from
the body
Effaced the young, growing buds from the potatoes' eyes,
Before placing them in the basket.

Two full baskets filled a hundredweight hessian sack,
But to be totally accurate, to satisfy the Ministry of Agriculture
regulations,
Each bag was weighed on the weighbridge placed by the side of
the pit.
After twenty bags were packed
My father took a packing needle with a curved eyelet
And painstakingly threaded it with binder twine,
Sewing the opening at the top in a neat, zig zag manner
While leaving handling grips at either end.

When every bag was securely sewn,
He grabbed each one by the rabbit, ears- like grips
And with a deft nudge of his knee against the midriff,
He expertly hoisted the sack into a waiting tractor-trailer.
And then transported the load to a storage barn in the
farmyard.

This whole process continued until
Five tons of potatoes were sorted, bagged
And ferried to their final collecting point.

The local potato-export merchant came, in a big lorry,
To take away one hundred bags of sweat and toil,
But more importantly, to produce a large bundle of crisp, white
five pound notes.
With quiet, happy smiles of complete satisfaction
My parents gratefully accepted this most welcome financial
reward.
For countless generations the potato has had a sentimental
attachment to Irish people.
For years it was the staple diet food of everyone.
But for many others, like my folks, it was and indeed is, their
regular, economic lifeline.

(3) Davagh Station

It was the final year at Primary school.
My turn had come to avail of a special morning treat.
One Friday, at half past seven, the Parish priest arrived at our house
In a black Volkswagen, beetle car.
He was collecting me to serve at the station Mass in Davagh -
an isolated area of my native parish,
Some seven miles away from the epicentre of all communal activity.
Because it was much closer, its inhabitants were forced to attend Sunday Mass, to go to school in a neighbouring parish.
A twice-yearly station was an official recognition of this unusual situation.

As we journeyed through the rustic, rolling countryside on a beautiful May morn,
The trees were bursting with blossoms, the green tubers beginning to conceal the brown, moulded soil of the potato drills.
The lush green fields were, intermittently, dotted with scores of cattle and sheep
As the delights of spring enveloped every townland in all their majestic beauty.
The host's house was freshly, neatly painted.
Its doors and windows glistened as the sun's rays progressively increased in strength, in length.

The whitewashed outhouses, the red, barn doors blended
perfectly
With the rambling rose bushes; the assorted lupins and sweet
William that adorned the front wall.

We entered the gravelled gateway; bordered on both sides by
tidily manicured, grass verges.
The people of Davagh were, justifiably, a proud race.
They may have been far away from the rest of us
But as they heartily welcomed the messenger of God, their
hearts, their minds exemplified the intense intimacy of their
Faith.
The priest was ushered into the kitchen
Where he heard each adult's Confession
Before he took out the sacred vessels, his vestments from the
Mass-kit case.
As he vested, twenty locals, dressed in their Sunday best, filled
the spacious sitting room, joyfully, excitedly, waiting for the
ceremony, their day of days to begin.

In those pre-Vatican Two years
The celebrant stood with his back to the people, saying Mass,
not in the vernacular, but in Latin.
Fr Cullen thus commenced with "Introibo ad altare Dei."
And I replied, "Ad Deum qui laetificat ad juventutem meam."
"I will go to the altar of God."
"To the God who giveth joy to my youth".
And so the introductory rite continued with alternating lines
Until the antiphon was completed and the Mass proper began.

When it was concluded, the temporary altar was transformed
Into part of a large, white-linen, covered dining table.
And the priest immediately, enthusiastically engaged in friendly
conversation
With the people of this extraordinarily welcoming, farming and
forestry community.
The varying prices of cattle in nearby Greencastle and
Draperstown
And the working conditions, in the adjacent coniferous state
forest, took centre stage.
Then all sat down to a bowl of hot porridge, tea, toast and fried
bread.
With a boiled egg for the man of the house, the priest and a
surprised, though humbled, yours truly.

After the breakfast was over, the men lit their pipes
And the women discussed the latest ladies' fashions and baby
news.
An hour later, the priest announced the arrangements for the
Autumn station.
As we drove homewards he explained to me
The historical tradition of the station Mass
And how it dated back to the terrible Penal times in Ireland.
And how the laity, under extremely difficult circumstances, had
kept alive the Christian message.
With the now rapid decline in religious vocations, their time to
do so again will surely come sooner rather than later.

(4) The Pick-up Baler

We stood at the corner of the hayfield
And watched, in joyful expectation,
As we observed for the first time,
A new, mechanical creation.
Propelled by a blue, Ford Dexta tractor
The pick-up baler had arrived!
Beginning its activity at the field's internal perimeter,
It gradually gobbled up the maze-like rows of hay, which
enveloped the whole field.

As the circular rows dwindled in number, shortened in length,
Our astonishment escalated, our disbelief intensified.
By the time the baler had reached the centre,
The rows of beautifully scented, new-mown hay had
disappeared.
They had been transformed into over two hundred, scattered
but tidily assembled, ready-made food parcels of hay.
Our winter fodder had appeared, incredibly, after one singular
procedure.
Suddenly, the vast, remaining surface area was barren and bare,
Except for the thousands of tiny, prickly stubbles, left behind by
the mowing machine.

Rectangular in shape, metal in composition,
The object of our attention was attached to two sets of rubber
wheels.
A line of tightly sprung but flexible prongs at the front

Quickly gathered up the rowed hay as the tractor was driven
along the outside of each row.
The revolving prongs flung the hay into the baler's central
chamber.
At regular intervals a large, moving knife cut off the supply
Before a ramming plunger compressed it
Into an ornately shaped, oblong bale of hay.

A mechanical knitter
Tightened two strands of twine
Around the freshly formed bundle,
To firmly secure the finished product.
With a loud, snapping, clicking sound,
Like a shot from a gun,
It was dispatched, at speed, out of the back of the baler
And onto the hard, newly-created, spacious ground behind it.

To all of us, it was a marvellous feat
On a par with man setting foot on the moon,
Or the later invention of a wireless, mobile phone.
More significantly, it was the answer to all our traditional,
haymaking worries.
The days of tedious, laborious, manual work were at an end.
No more continuous hand-raking, pitchforking into ricks,
No more building hay pikes or storing never-ending heaps of
loose hay into dusty, windswept haysheds.
One entrepreneurial invention had eliminated the drudgery of
the past and made future haymaking fun for all.

The bales were temporarily stacked in the field;
Two at a time, criss-crossed on the top of each other, in sixes,
With knots in and down
To protect them against the adverse effects of wind and rain.
After a few weeks' seasoning
They were collected, drawn by tractor and trailer
And packed closely together, in a hayshed.
For us this was sheer heaven, pure undiluted, extended
playtime.

Every autumn a field full of potato pits,
A garden with perfectly manicured corn stacks
And a hayshed crammed to the rafters with good quality hay
Were the ultimate in farmers' satisfaction in the 1960's and
1970's.
But unlike the potatoes and corn, the arrival of the hay bales
Meant that the season's hay work was essentially over.
The daily feeding of cattle with hay during the winter,
regardless of its severity,
Was merely a physical and social exercise in enjoyment, an
outlet for our youthful, surplus energy.

(5)   Slieve Gallion Braes

"My name is James McGarvey and I'll have you understand
I come from Derrygennard and I own a farm of land.
But the rents are getting higher and I can no longer stay.
So farewell unto you, bonny, bonny Slieve Gallion Braes."

In the mid nineteenth century, the composer of that most
haunting of emigration ballads,
Had to leave his native land, not because of unemployment,
But due to the cruelty of excessive taxes,
Imposed by an uncaring, greedy landlord.
The selfishness of this man meant that
The Lissan farmer would never have the financial freedom
To settle down, marry the girl that he loved best,
On the banks, the braes of his native Slieve Gallion,
A place of consummate beauty, a district of rare splendour,
A place that he lovingly called home.

Situated amidst the parishes of Desertmartin, Lissan and
Ballinascreen,
Its summit is a flat-topped, basalt cairn, a tamac of architectural
expertise,
Where Callan, the grandson of the High King, Colla Uais, is
buried.
Its spectacular, panoramic, viewing balcony
Fascinates all who have stood on its hallowed peak
And stared, in awesome wonder, for miles in every direction.

It has to be one of the greatest expanses of uninterrupted beauty,
Anywhere on the island of Ireland.
Amazingly, on a bright, sunny, cloudless day, six counties of Ulster
Are clearly outlined in all their graceful elegance, their most defining characteristics.

To the east, one can easily identify the dominating Belfast hills,
the linear Glens of Antrim brushing against the horizon.
Fronting these, the remnants of an extinct volcano
With regular, steep sides crowned by a circular plateau;
Thus stands Slemish, like a watchtower proudly presiding,
Reminding everyone of its most famous past pupil—the enslaved boy called Patrick.
To the southeast, sixty miles away, lofty Slieve Donard leads its Mourne colleagues, blending effortlessly into the Down skyline.
To the northwest the equidistant Bluestacks of Donegal enhance and balance the binocular view.
In between, the majestic Sawel - the King of the Sperrins-
Loiters high across the border amidst Derry and Tyrone,
Carefully observing Slieve Gallion, its little sister, its most endearing eastern summit.

Like a patchwork quilt of multiple colours,
Acre upon acre of green, leafy potatoes, yellow-glistening corn, ripening barley heads,
In neatly tailored, irregular patterned fields,
Herds of Friesian cattle, Suffolk sheep, grazing peacefully,

Richly embellish the summer landscape on every side.
Sitting happily, comfortably amongst the assorted collage, is the
largest freshwater lake in these islands.
Sweet Lough Neagh, in its calm, gleaming entirety, surrounded
by five counties,
A shining jewel in a green belt that welcomes the meandering
Bann, threading its way to the Atlantic between Portstewart and
Castlerock;
While the small, adjacent urban settlements of Moneymore,
Desertmartin and Draperstown tastefully complement
The long lens snapshot of the more populated Cookstown with
its striking, lengthy, Main Street fading into the heartlands of
Tyrone.

As Slieve Gallion gradually slopes down to the pasture lands
below,
A maze of delightful coniferous woodlands, lakes, rivers,
percolate its twisting, turning perimeter.
On one side, Carndaisy Glen and Iniscarn forest display stately
trees of resplendent beauty;
Their regal formations of sitka spruce, pine, oak, enriching the
surrounding vegetation.
On the opposite periphery, on a hill in the townland of
Ballybriest, the remains of Neolithic cairn graves are firmly
entrenched,
Reminding us of a storied past, clouded by the passing of time.
That old cemetery possesses a classical, double court tomb
which
Overlooks, in a descending chain of magnificence,

The quiet ambience of Lough Fea, a mountain lake providing
solace, comfort to the visiting picnicking tourist,
As well as, pragmatically, releasing one hundred and eighty
acres of water to thousands of consumers in two counties.

Because of the callous insensitivity of others, James McGarvey
had to leave
A blanket bog of breathtaking flora, rare wildlife:
The Irish hare, the curlew, the red grouse and the otter being
among its prized inhabitants.
Never again would he see the excited crowds of people
Arriving from his own and neighbouring parishes
To celebrate the two social highlights of his year:
The midsummer festival of bonfire night in June,
The picking of the greyish-blue blaeberries on blaeberry
Sunday in August.
Like James, many young people today have to leave their
homelands because of man's inhumanity to man.
Like him they, too, share the same sad sentiments of his last
goodbye.

"Farewell to Old Ireland, that island of green,
To the parish of Lissan, and the cross of Ballinascreen.
May God shine upon you when I am far away
And a long farewell onto you bonny, bonny, Slieve Gallion
Braes.

(6) The Day of the Threshing

One early Autumn morning,
Six men from our neighbourhood arrived on the street
For the communal highlight of the farming year
-The day of the threshing
It was my father's turn for the morrowing or meitheal,
A long-established custom whereby neighbours came together,
in rural Ireland,
To help each other with a labour-intensive seasonal, agricultural
activity.
The annual threshing fell into such a category.

We, as young children, were especially delighted to witness
This ancient co-operative, mutually reciprocated system.
In an era of little community interaction, it provided a welcome
and exciting diversion,
From the normally mundane, then somewhat lonely chores of
daily, country life.
When Bertie Bell, the Thresher man, came up the lane, on his
Ford Major tractor,
Along with a high, pink, Garvie threshing machine
And a large baler hitched behind,
All this was changed: we were now hosts of our own exclusive
farming show.

Bertie parked the different agricultural machinery
Alongside the conically-shaped, well - tailored corn stacks,
In the garden in front of the house.
After an informal conference with the rest of the men,

It was decided which threshing portfolios would be allocated to whom.

Our roles would be peripheral to the main event.

We would be available, as messengers, amongst the various workers.

That aside, we would, in essence, just be whole-hearted interested spectators.

Threshing was a complex yet simple operation.

The harvested crop was fed into the top of the thresher

Where the good grain seed of the heads of the sheaves were separated from the useless chaff.

And both of these were disconnected from the yellow stalks.

The newly threshed grain was collected in two hundred weight bags at the back of the thresher.

The threshed, loose straw was coughed up outside the front of the machine

Before two men briskly forked it into the baler,

Parked about twelve feet ahead of it.

Operations commenced after the Thresher man

Connected a wide, long drive belt from the thresher to the tractor and switched on the engine.

Two workers took the rush thatch off the corn stack

And proceeded to quickly toss the sheaves onto a platform at the top of the thresher.

Here another man cut the straps of each sheaf with a knife.

His companion then spread out the stalks like a fan

And gently fed the opened head of each sheaf

Into the rapid, revolving, serrated jams of the machine's entrails.

The feeder's job was the most dangerous of all.
It required delicate handling skills, patience and total concentration,
Otherwise, one small slip could have fatal implications.
When the threshing was completed the nagging, humming drone of the thresher stopped,
And for the first time, in many hours, human voices could be heard again.
The bags of corn, the bales of straw were stored in the nearby barn.
The chaff was swept up for disposal at a later date.
And my mother called everyone in for a well-earned roast meat dinner.

After the meal was consumed
Bertie and his fascinating machinery headed off down the lane.
The following day would see him resume hostilities,
On the farm across the road.
The same workers would return
To perform the same tasks;
Just a different venue with different children,
Experiencing their day of the year.

Meanwhile we looked on in sadness,
That our wonderful day had ended.
Fido, the dog, followed the Thresher man
Down the lane, stopped at the bottom
And barked a friendly farewell.
He, too, had a fantastic day,
Chasing dozens of startled mice
As they scurried from their winter hibernation in the warm,
protective custody of the corn stacks.

(7)   Leaving Home

As I tried to sleep, my initial whole-hearted enthusiasm
Began to undulate, and then wane with an increasing sense of
loneliness.
I was leaving the security, the familiarity of home
For a journey into the unknown, far away in a strange place,
surrounded by strange people.
Conversely, I was eagerly looking forward
To the double challenges of learning different subjects, of
playing more sport.
But socially I would, undoubtedly, miss my family, the friends
who came on their céili,
The intimate "bits and pieces" of everyday life would be but a
distant memory.

In the early afternoon I said goodbye to the lush, green fields,
the peacefully grazing cattle.
I looked longingly at the beautifully-crafted stooks of yellow
corn in the roadside field.
And the impressively built pikes of hay that adorned the garden
in front of the house.
But, I meditated, was this just foolish sentimentality
Which I had decided to forego
While following my dream in a college almost thirty miles away?
For the umpteenth time, my lonely mother checked the
contents of my suit case
And kept reminding me that she would really be looking
forward to my weekly letters with all the news.

With my father, we set off in our friend's Morris car.

After about an hour's driving, we had already passed through Cookstown, Dungannon and The Moy.

Then the famed, imposing twin spires of Saint Patrick's Cathedral appeared on the horizon.

As we neared the ecclesiastical capital,

They progressively towered higher and higher in the bright September sky,

Until they completely dominated the Armagh landscape.

I was becoming more nervous now, unsure as my eyes started to well up.

But I proudly kept my outward stoicism, my calm demeanour, and my natural reticence.

We entered the Cathedral gateway, sped up the winding driveway,

Around the corner and there it stood - Saint Patrick's College!

Its grey, sombre walls intersected symmetrically with a countless number of windows.

Its grim exterior reflected my inner turmoil making me wish I had not come.

The car stopped and a Senior boy escorted us to the students' entrance before being greeted by the Dean of Discipline.

Dutiful pleasantries were perfunctorily reciprocated.

My father, head down, turned quickly away after rushing to say his goodbye.

I, momentarily, looked back at his disappearing figure, almost imploringly, before rapidly retreating into the "big boys don't cry syndrome"

Two rows of neatly arranged beds filled the dormitory.

Each student was allocated a bedside locker and a wardrobe space.

A line of spotlessly clean, wash hand basins occupied the top wall.

I was the first incumbent – the only recruit in situ.

I unpacked all my personal belongings, took out the freshly starched, white, stiff sheets.

Labels had been sewn on them and my name written, with my mother's distinctive cursive script, in black, indelible ink.

For the first time in my life I really, properly, made my own bed.

This was a definite symbolising gesture to my newly acquired, though reluctant, independent status!

The eerie silence, the weird emptiness were abruptly interrupted

By the lively, loud arrival of two other first years with high-pitched Belfast accents.

Unable to cope with their perceived differences, their apparent total happiness,

I slipped quietly away, went down the stairs, along the main corridor before drifting outside.

For ages I just stood, wondering and worrying, beside the iron railings that faced the tennis courts.

Beyond them lay a myriad of assorted rooftops, billowing, smoking chimneys

Which comprised the urban sprawl that was Armagh City.

And I thought to myself, what am I doing here?

My father would now be telling my mother
How he left me in good fettle, without a worry in the world.
My siblings would be playing marbles or throwing rings at a
board in the kitchen
Or listening to our regular Monday night visitor relating the
latest instalment of the local retired, married couple
Who, after selling a herd of cattle, once ordered, in a
Cookstown café,
One bowl of soup and two spoons for their dinner!
The reality, the finality of my fated, Summer decision
Was beginning to haunt, to infuriate me.

Unexpectedly, a third year student, accompanied by his first
year brother, disturbed my reverie.
He asked me my name and proceeded to tell
That my mother had asked his mother for him to look out for
me.
They had been old school friends in the neighbouring parish of
Kildress, many years previously.
Immediately, I was rejuvenated as the kindly, thoughtful James
Doris
Escorted the "two preps" to the refectory
Where we had our first boarding school meal of bread, butter
and watery jam.
The gloom of despondency had miraculously lifted: the spring
in my step had increased enormously.

To copper fasten my new-found confidence,
I discovered that the student prefect in charge of our dormitory
Was a fellow GAA supporter from my own native county.
And who was sitting beside us at the table
But my erstwhile Belfast, first year acquaintances.
They generously offered us chocolate, sweets and more
importantly, their unqualified friendship.
Suddenly, homesickness, negativity had disappeared.
The next morning could not come quickly enough.

(8)   The Dean's Morning Call

One of the main, negative characteristics of boarding school life
Was an occasional sense of loneliness, a feeling of total isolation.
In my experience, imposed periods of compulsory silence,
Such as the time between night prayers until breakfast the
following morning,
Tended to reinforce this conviction.
I remember this austerity measure was only officially broken by
the Dean's intercession
When, each morning of our school lives, the dormitory door
suddenly burst open
And he walked in, furiously ringing a handbell.

This was the automatic signal, the rule book said,
For students to immediately arise from their slumber,
Stand upright to attention, barefooted on the cold, hard floor.
The tall, cheery cleric would loudly greet us
With a distinctive, spiritual salutation in Latin.
"Benedicamus Domino" was his blessing,
To which we were expected to answer
In an equally, clear voice, our grateful response - "Deo Gratias".

Some had great difficulty in getting up at once
Or properly verbalising the response.
So the Dean would repeat the mantra louder and louder,
As he stared at the individual(s) before quickly striding past.
Indeed, it was not unusual for such a student

To catch his toe on the bottom of his pyjamas leg,
Then stumble awkwardly onto the floor
Before mumbling a rather jumbled version of the correct reply!

As the swinging bell's intensity decreased,
The swishing, black, soutane-clad figure disappeared
To repeat the same ritual in every other dormitory.
Each student now knelt down, by his bedside, to say his prayers,
Then splashed, washed and dressed in the deadly, vocal
stillness,
Before joining the rest of the student body
In the college chapel for morning Mass
And the last leg of the dreaded, silence quarantine.

Nowadays, schooldays have changed: changed utterly beyond
recognition.
Our student successors have no boarding; no freezing, cold
floors anywhere.
Compulsory silence is a historic phrase; daily Mass an aged,
adult preserve.
They are well fed; and ferried to and from school each day.
They have been given more resources; the latest technology is
always at hand.
We were extremely resilient, exceptionally thrifty, and deeply
appreciative.
Only time will tell whether or not they will be any happier;
Whether they will make our country a better place to live and
work in.

(9)   The Royal Showband

Along with five other final year, secondary students,
I obtained my first weekly pay of two pounds, at the start of
July,
For the annual Diocesan Priests' retreat in our old Alma Mater.
The job specification included serving three daily meals
And acting as a general factotum for the assembled men of the
cloth.
For us this experience was an incredible sea change, a welcome
difference,
Compared to the subservience, the authoritarianism of a few
weeks earlier.
A sense of freedom, mutual respect, an appreciation of our true
worth pervaded the conclave.

A kind, friendly priest acknowledged our importance best
By presenting us with complimentary tickets, a chauffeur –
driven car
To his big mid-week dance in Portadown – a then musical
Mecca of showband land.
Indeed, this magnanimous gesture could aptly be described
As our induction, our transition from the boys-only world of
innocent, raw teenagers,
To the great, outside environment of work, music, third level,
dancing, girls.
Thanks to his innate understanding of youthful exuberance,
We would be seeing Ireland's leading dancing artists - the Royal
Showband.

When we arrived inside the centre of our new universe
We made our way up to the balcony,
Where we had a panoramic all-night view of the seven-piece
band on stage; the gyrating punters on the floor.
Looking, listening, learning, was a fascinating, wonderful
adventure for all of us,
As we watched hundreds of happy, radiant faces
Go backwards, forwards, up and down, in and out
To the magical beat and rocking rhythm of a majestic
showband.
The trailblazers from County Waterford were really
outperforming our already high expectations.

As the band leader called, "Next dance, please,"
The women, in their beehive hairstyles, gathered on one side;
the men, in winklepicker shoes on the other.
There was a stampede of Grand National proportions
As the men dashed across the floor to select a dancing partner.
Some of the chosen were delighted, others meekly accepted,
While the disillusioned, the disenfranchised, disappeared to the
back of the hall or the cloakroom.
It was all a tad indisciplined, momentarily uncivilised.
But when the music struck up, harmony soon ruled, new
friendships were created, old ones rekindled, romances
commenced.

The melodic versatility, the sheer quality of all the musicians,
held us spellbound.
The brass section, the guitar ensemble played in perfect tune
As the three vocalists, whether separately or in unison,

Splendidly sang the complete spectrum of music's vast genre.
Nevertheless, it was the uniquely talented, lead vocalist Brendan
Bowyer
Who overwhelmingly captured our hearts, our minds.
True, band leader, Tom Dunphy was an outstanding country
singer
But Brendan Bowyer really was our first and one of our
greatest-ever pop stars.

His athleticism, the energy that he expended on stage,
To complement the tremendous range of his vocal ability, was
truly phenomenal.
To be able to switch immediately, seamlessly,
From heart-rending Irish ballads such as "Boolavogue" and
"The Croppy Boy"
To the rhythm-and-blues classic, "My Boy Lollipop" was a
remarkable achievement.
His impersonation of the full repertoire of Elvis Presley's songs
Was so good, so real, that Presley himself loved nothing better
Than, to watch, in later years, Bowyer cover his songs when he
was in concert in Las Vegas.

As our world premiere of the showband scene drew to a close,
Hundreds of people gathered around the stage,
Looking to talk to, have autographs signed or photographs
taken with their superstars, their cult heroes.
The concluding words of Tom Dunphy echoed distinctly
through the hall

"From the Royal Showband, County Waterford,
It is good night, God Bless
And remember, if you are driving,
It is better to arrive home five minutes late than to be dead on
time!"

Our taxi man brought back to Armagh,
A group of very happy, satisfied students.
It was the first of many such journeys for all of us
Throughout the length and breadth of Ireland and, indeed,
beyond.
For me, it was the beginning of an all-embracing love of
showbands that has lasted to this day.
Though two pounds may have been a paltry wage
It was the catalyst, which introduced us to a genial, thoughtful,
young padre
And provided me with an eternal, invaluable source of fabulous
entertainment.

(10) In Memoriam – A Fermanagh Friend

Our first day of lectures at the Training College had just ended.
After a thoroughly, enjoyable, wholesome evening meal,
A group of us – old friends and new – exchanged pleasantries
And some very positive, mutual opinions were shared on the
dramatic changes in our educational lifestyles.
We then retired to the residents' lounge
Where we played records, including an LP of the late pop star,
Buddy Holly,
On a record player which had definitely seen better days.
But we all felt good, relaxed and free for the first time in our
lives as we listened intently to such iconic songs as "Rave On"
and "Peggy Sue".

Suddenly the door burst open and in walked an old secondary
school colleague
Who had been two years ahead of me.
Renowned as a friendly mentor, of every student, regardless of
age or year,
He was in a particularly buoyant, self-satisfied mood.
Himself a talented footballer he had, because of injury, been
forced to sit out a training session
Conducted by the head of the College's PE department
And former Derry All-Ireland final captain, Jim McKeever,
Nationally acknowledged as one of the all-time greats of Gaelic
football.

The first Gaelic Footballer of the Year was actually playing in
his own coaching session.
And on this specific evening he was so impressive in the art of
spectacular high fielding
That my erstwhile friend was immediately prompted
To tell us first years that we should see for ourselves a unique
footballing artist in action.
"I know Buddy Holly was good but he is dead.
Would you ever come out to the football field
And see a real live individual performance
By an exponent at his imperious best?"

Then the witty, perceptive third year added,
"McKeever is so good tonight and jumping so high
That he is actually catching flying angels coming down from
heaven!"
We dutifully, obediently, trudged out onto the playing pitch.
Sure enough the assessment was deadly accurate.
We were lucky to see a   master footballer
Performing to the zenith of his considerable athletic ability,
For, probably, the last time in a star-studded career which had
now entered the twilight zone.

Having gone our separate ways, Stephen McGarrity and I did
not meet again
Until over twenty-five years later in a shopping centre in
Enniskillen.
We stopped, chatted animatedly, sentimentally recalling the
past,

But looking forward with renewed hope to the future.
Unfortunately, our immediate personal commitments curtailed our conversation.
But we dutifully promised to formally meet again within the year.
Sadly, however, he was struck down with a sudden illness
And died shortly afterwards in the prime of life.

Whether it was a lonely first year,
Walking along a secondary school corridor on a dark,
November evening,
Or anyone, anywhere, he always had the instinctive ability to make everyone feel good about themselves.
He, invariably, had his priorities in the right order.
For Stephen people came first, second, and always.
After all, it was his innate desire to share a moment of sporting excellence
That was the catalytic icebreaker,
 For making me feel so much at home all those years ago.

Section B

BLOODY SUNDAY TRILOGY:
A Defining Microcosm of Northern Ireland's
Core Problem.

(11) The March

Happily leaving their homes, some never to return,
Hundreds of Derry's finest men
Marched towards the forbidden centre
Of their stolen seat of power in Guildhall Square.
Decades of wilful neglect, gross injustices
And now, internment without trial,
Empowered them to seek a future
Of equal opportunity and prosperity for all.

But the imperial might of a diminishing empire thought otherwise.
Trampling on the rights of "their Irish subordinates" to walk the
planned route,
Ruthlessly chasing unarmed civilians
With their powerful Saracens, their deadly guns.
"Croppies lie down. Remember, you are underlings",
Seemed to be the dominant, domineering message
As a frightened people fled for safety
To avoid the threatening, wicked weaponry of impending death.

Running alongside the priest whose handkerchief of peace
Is flashed across the world,
Every time this horrible day is recalled,
Was young Jackie Duddy,
Shot in the back as he desperately tried to seek refuge
In the courtyard of Rossville flats.
The first fatal victim of the Parachute Regiment's day of shame.
The first innocent to be slain in cold blood.

"I am going to die, doctor, am I?"
William McKinney plaintively whispered,
As the gentle, sensitive Raymond McClean momentarily offered
hope.

"You'll probably be alright if we can get you quickly to hospital".
Minutes later, Father Mulvey administered the Last Rites.
William spoke no more
And slipped into unconsciousness,
Before confirming his own last, prophetic words.

Thirteen fallen heroes lay dead
On the streets of their native city;
Many others seriously injured as flying bullets pierced the tender
limbs
Of terrified youths, frantically trying to escape from danger.
Alternating thoughts of anger and hopelessness
Ransacked the minds of fifteen thousand participants;
Suddenly suffering the most intimidating experience
Of a lifetime of cruel, endless negativity.

On Monday morning the deserted city streets
Echoed silently to the terrible events of the previous afternoon;
In tandem, the empty, heavy hearts and broken spirits of besieged
citizens
Left everyone speechless, feeling almost forgotten.
Thankfully, the world's press came
To seek truthful answers to searching questions
Which would gradually enable a resilient people
To come to terms with their darkest hour.

Someday, somehow, a vibrant, risen race
Would surely take their rightful place
Amongst a fairer society built on justice, fraternity, and equality.
Someday, somehow, those who had prematurely left this world
Would, proudly and unblemished, walk hand in hand
And stand shoulder to shoulder with the rest of us,
When a new, rekindled, revitalised Derry
And a more beautiful, happier tomorrow would finally come to pass.

(12) The Funeral

Sitting, silently, uneasily in an old battered railway carriage
From Belfast to Derry,
We journeyed to Ireland's most discriminated city
On its saddest, most poignant occasion.

The previous evening thirteen coffined young men
Were brought from their devastated homes,
Along winding lamp-lit pathways,
In solemn, separate processions to St Mary's Church in
Creggan.

All night, large crowds from Derry, Donegal, Tyrone and
beyond
Came to pay their prayerful respects,
To a truly courageous group of innocent men,
Cruelly cut down in the prime of life.

The panoramic view of the River Foyle
Nestled snugly beneath the church when we arrived at the
hilltop.
Thousands of worried, tearful mourners thronged the nearby
rain-laden streets
On that cold, dismal, February morning.

All Nationalist Ireland, official and ordinary,
Were there in massive numbers.
Most others were then either unable or unwilling
To appreciate the intensity of the communal hurt felt by their
fellow citizens.

Thirteen identical coffins, placed side by side,
Facing the altar in the church's sanctuary,
Was an overwhelming, disconcerting experience,
Too difficult to accept, too emotional to control.

Why, oh why, had anyone been asked
To bear such a huge personal burden?
Why, oh why, did a continuously downtrodden community
Have to suffer such humiliation, such tragedy?

Though entirely incidental,
The beautiful liturgical music of the Requiem Mass
Blended perfectly with the natural and incremental weeping of
the bereaved
As the ceremony unfolded.

When the roll call of the deceased was read,
We realised, for the first time, the vast significance of what had
happened.
Suddenly, an eerie silence descended as priests and people
United in spiritual recollection.

The finality of death was never so stark, never so heartbreaking
As the haunting, lyrical strains of "Nearer My God To Thee"
Accompanied the mortal remains of the victims
On their last trip - to the cemetery.

We returned to the train station for our homeward journey.
Cold in body and colder in spirit.
Somewhere between Coleraine and Ballymoney
The future of our troubled land became crystal clear.

A catalytic moment had arrived.
No one who could have prevented all of this
Really understood the complexities,
The various challenges of the Orange and the Green, the
differences between Britain and Ireland.

The course of the conflict was now altered, irretrievably,
And not for the better.
Violence and counter violence, not consultation and consensus,
Would be the more likely future scenario.

Many more years of terrible tragedies, appalling atrocities,
surely awaited.
Before people of real vision could emerge
To mend broken hearts, change contrasting minds
In the process of uniting a divided people.

(13) Vindicated

Officially proclaiming the total innocence of the guiltless,
Blaming the paratroopers for wrongfully killing and injuring
Fleeing, unarmed civilians,
David Cameron stood at the Westminster dispatch desk.

Continuing the integrity, the honesty initiated years earlier by
Tony Blair,
He told the world he was deeply sorry
For the unjustified and unjustifiable actions
Of British soldiers on the streets of Derry in 1972.

No marcher on that fateful day
Posed either a threat of causing death or serious injury.
The Paras, recklessly, lost control, inventing incredible,
untruthful stories
To exonerate their own deplorable deeds.

Just prior to that historic announcement
The families of those shot on Bloody Sunday
Symbolically, walked the same route
That their relatives should have taken all those years ago.

The re-enactment over, they were led into the Guildhall
Where, ironically, they were so often denied access.
After personally hearing the positive results of the Saville
enquiry,
They, spontaneously, ran outside relieved, elated and
completely overcome with joyous expectation.

In the square they joined thousands of excited, exhilarated
Supporters and friends, who were watching,
On a giant television screen, David Cameron
Telling them what they wanted, for years, to hear.

Those heroic Derry victims are role models for peace in their
own right.
Thanks to their ultimate sacrifices and
The loyalty of those who, fearlessly, stood by them,
Justice has, at last, been done.

On June 15th, 2010,
The dreams of those who laboured so faithfully were fulfilled.
The people have now been set free; from the millstones of fear;
the demons of discrimination and innuendo.
A beautiful, new tomorrow has arrived. Deo Gratias.

Section C

THIRTY YEARS OF CONFLICT:
Ballymurphy Killings.
Loyalist and Republican Days of Shame.
Good Friday Agreement.

(14) A Near Escape

Walking down the Whiterock Road,
Casually chatting, to a teaching colleague,
About the prospects of our school football team,
Dramatically disturbed by a woman
On the other side of the road,
Shrieking animatedly,
"Would youse lie down on the footpath – quickly?"
Before hastily disappearing into the nearby housing estate.

Suddenly, mysteriously, the normally busy road
Became totally devoid of traffic or people.
Her voice had sounded ominous;
Her words, alarmingly, terse and clipped.
So, we quickly obeyed.
Within minutes we understood why.
The unmistakeable rat a tat-tat of a machine gun
Rent the air with a terrifying velocity.

Seconds later, from the opposite direction,
Across a wasteland, gunfire was returned with equal venom.
For what appeared an eternity, a battle ensued between the
military and the paramilitary.
And we were unwilling, unsighted, ringside spectators.
Trying to quietly mumble the Act of Contrition.
Failed, as the words would not release themselves from my
increasingly dry palate.
So, I hoped that God would save us
From the limbo-land between life and death.

A thousand childhood memories flashed through the mind,
Homely images of family occasions adorned the imagination.
Why had I left the tranquillity of rural Derry
To find myself amidst the horror of urban guerrilla warfare?
We looked sideways at each other, wordless, worrying.
Our only diversion - the constant clicking and creaking of his bicycle wheel,
Revolving in its new-found prostrate position
And I thinking, "A drop of oil would not have gone astray".

Just as speedily as it began, the skirmish ended
And the watchful woman came back
And told us the coast was clear.
Instantaneously, magically, both traffic and people re-appeared
As if nothing untoward had occurred.
We rose, gingerly, to our feet
And peeked, surreptitiously,
Over the concrete, boundary wall.

A lone, camouflaged gunman
Cowered in the thick undergrowth,
Before crawling away over the field.
We wiped our foreheads, settled our minds, and steadied our feet.
Only the breadth of a fence had separated us from the line of fire.
Someone had been praying for us.
Otherwise, we would just have been two additional statistics.
On the Roll Call of the dead during the Troubles.

(15) Ballymurphy

Resting in the sloping shadows of the Black Mountain,
A typical example of structured, social deprivation,
A long- term victim of discriminatory practices,
A regular casualty of violence - both invasive and reactionary.
Yet you had a human heart of gold,
An all-embracing mentality, infectious in its warmth and
friendliness,
Remaining continually positive in attitude,
Though, in essence, seriously disadvantaged.

But three August days in 1971
Were to herald a decisive downturn
As your world was torn asunder,
By bureaucratic insensitivity, by military might.
When an innocent man from Crossmaglen
Was shot dead by the British army
Because his van accidentally backfired at a police station;
Belfast, instantly, became an angry, riotous, burning inferno.

Two days later, many Nationalist communities
Were awakened early by the pre-arranged signal
Of dustbin lids banging on street pavements.
Hundreds of people, from only one side of the sectarian divide,
Were dragged from their homes and interned without trial.
The Stormont government had decided,
In their selective wisdom, that no Unionist
Should endure such treatment, such humiliation.

No one suffered more than you,
As crowds of soldiers saturated the whole area

With their tanks, their guns, their checkpoints, their raids.
Nobody was left untouched
By this inhuman behaviour, this moral depravity.
Within the next forty eight hours, eleven of your citizens
Were, tragically, killed by the invading parachute regiment.
A pall of desperate gloom filled the air.

As he stood opposite the army base, Daniel Teggart,
With multiple wounds, fatally shot.
Mother of eight, Joan Connolly, killed
As she tended the mortally wounded Noel Phillips.
Catholic curate, Fr Hugh Mullan, shot dead
Waving a white handkerchief as he anointed an injured man,
Are but a sample snapshot of what happened
To all the others whose lives were so brutally extinguished.

This really was Belfast's Bloody Sunday,
Your Armageddon of despair, terror and death.
One wonders if the parachute regiment
Had been properly disciplined after this,
Would the people of Derry, six months later,
Have had to experience
Their January nightmare,
Their day of unforgettable grief?

I have lived and worked amongst you
For seven years of highs and lows,
Wonderful enjoyment, sincerity, camaraderie.
You gave me my first job,
You earned me my first pay.
Part of you then made me what I am today.
Some day you too will rejoice
After a terrible wrong is corrected, after natural justice is
accomplished.

(16) Springhill 1972

Father Kevin Donnelly was having his evening meal.
Suddenly, two very distressed, concerned visitors burst in,
Telling him several people had been shot and badly wounded,
A short distance away in Springhill estate.
As he was about to leave,
His fellow curate, Father Noel Fitzpatrick,
Came back to the house, told him to finish his meal
And that he would attend to the emergency sick call.

Shortly before this, from their billet post
High up, in a nearby timber yard, overlooking the whole
Springhill area,
British army marksmen started to fire, indiscriminately,
numerous shots
Into the adjacent, sprawling streets.
Consequently, as they were speaking to their friends
And without any reason or warning,
Two completely innocent youngsters,
16-year-old John Dougal and 13-year-old Margaret Gargan,
were killed by the gunfire.

Accompanied by two parishioners,
Father of six, Patrick Butler
And 15-year-old schoolboy, David McCafferty,
The calm, dutiful Father Fitzpatrick hurried to the scene.
Waving a white handkerchief

And dressed in his normal clerical clothes,
He swiftly quickened his pace as he saw another injured youth,
Lying prostrate in the middle of Westrock Drive.

When he went to administer the Last Rites,
An army sniper rapidly fired a single bullet.
This penetrated the priest's head,
Before entering Patrick Butler's body, killing both of them instantly.
Young David McCafferty, rushing to help his fallen companions,
Was then, mercilessly, also shot dead.
The official custodians of justice
Had, heartlessly, killed five unarmed individuals.

On that lovely, sunny, July evening,
Less than a year after eleven other people,
In the same parish,
Died in tragically similar circumstances,
Unnecessary death had once again visited a tortured, heartbroken locality.
Surely the afflicted and bereaved people of Springhill
Deserve unequivocal justice and moral recompense so that
Some satisfactory closure can be brought to their long-lasting grief.

Hearing the sad news of the fatalities,
Fr Donnelly arrived to anoint
Those, including Fr Fitzpatrick, who had been killed.

How difficult, how poignant this all must have been
For this most gracious, this most warm-hearted of men
Who, for over sixty more years,
Was to fulfil a long and faithful ministry
In various parts of his native diocese.

This is something he might not have had
But for the thoughtfulness and self-sacrifice
Of a dear, departed friend.
Still, there was no more able or compassionate conduit
For the unexpectedly bereaved than the same Fr Donnelly,
As he eased the journey of the victims across the Rubicon,
From the trials and tribulations of this life
To the joys and comforts of the next.

Hopefully, those in authority will one day soon similarly ease
The anguish of those dearest and nearest to them,
That they suddenly, and without time to say goodbye, left
behind
With only the thoughts of what might have been
To reflect and ponder on
During the many sad days and long nights of their shattered
lives.

(17) Senator Paddy Wilson
– A Friend To All

The phone rang at eight thirty on a summer evening:
"I am delayed at the City Hall.
I won't be able to attend tonight's meeting.
Will see you soon".

Just a typical routine call
From a politician, unable to be
In two places, at the one time.
We would see him at the next meeting, or so we thought.

Four hours later his badly mutilated body
Along with a friend's, similarly dismembered,
Was left at a quarry,
On the Hightown Road in North Belfast.

Abducted by a paramilitary gang
In a frenetic, frenzied attack.
Cruelly tortured in barbaric fashion
Before being eventually assassinated.

Poor genial, gentle Paddy Wilson
Removed from this world
Because he was a Catholic, an SDLP member,
A believer in the unity of Ireland - only by mutual consent.

Merely a few weeks earlier many of us
Had happily traversed the streets of West Belfast
Joking and laughing, with Paddy on his way,
To another outstanding local election success.

Thinking of speaking to a good friend,
Thinking of what happened to him so shortly afterwards,
Still rankles, still hurts, sends even now,
Frightening shivers down one's spine.

This was a mere cameo of what happened
To over three thousand people.
But for his wife Brigid, son Paul and whole family circle
It was the earthly end of the man they knew and loved so well.

We carried him up the Falls
Past his old electoral stomping ground,
Before laying him to rest in Milltown cemetery.
Farewell, dear friend. You really were a true and trusted
confidant.

A powerful advocate for the underprivileged, the elderly.
We will always remember you with kindness, with fondness.
And after your last phone call - some sadness, tinged with a
mighty pride
For having known one of Belfast's great human beings.

(18) David Ervine
– A Loyalist Visionary

It was the worst day
Of the worst year of the Troubles.
Known as Bloody Friday,
Nine people were killed and one hundred and thirty badly
injured,
As the Provisional IRA detonated twenty-two bombs
Right across the city of Belfast.
On this day of his 19th birthday
One young Protestant had had enough.

After witnessing the horrific mutilation
Of so much human life,
The terrible destruction of his native city's infrastructure,
David Ervine decided to join a loyalist paramilitary organisation
So that he could properly defend his community,
As he saw it,
Against the gunmen and bombers
Of extreme Irish Republicanism.

For the next few years
He was actively involved in a counter campaign
To dethrone the IRA from their policy
Of bombing economic, security and political targets.
One Autumn day this working lifestyle ended abruptly
When he was stopped driving a stolen car containing explosives.

Later he was charged, convicted and sentenced
To eleven years of imprisonment for possession of explosives
with intent to endanger life.

Being in prison allowed him plenty of time for reflection and
self-analysis.
There he met a well-known convicted loyalist
Who now believed in constitutional politics as the only way
forward.
The young Ervine was greatly impressed by his new-found
mentor.
After being released, he joined a political party.
By 1998, he and his party had played a constructive role
In the signing of the Good Friday Agreement.
The conversion from a paramilitary past to a peaceful, political
future was complete.

Even when some loyalists would sometimes doubt
The validity of the settlement,
David remained steadfast to its abiding principles.
He realised that the only means of meaningful advancement
Was for unionist, loyalist, nationalist, republican,
To work together to accommodate
Each other's political philosophies
In a spirit of tolerance and reconciliation.

As well as being pivotal to the implementation of the loyalist
ceasefire
He became a champion of conflict resolution,

Respected and admired throughout the free world.
This most eloquent of politicians
Was a tireless advocate of progressive politics.
He was a man of honour, courage, vision,
Always prepared to change if he deemed it necessary
For all the people of Northern Ireland.

Sadly, he died in the prime of life in 2007.
Let his own words be his everlasting and most appropriate of
epitaphs:
"The politics of division see thousands of people dead
And headstones on the graves of young men.
We have been fools.
Let us not be fools any longer."
David Ervine learned from and accepted past mistakes.
All politicians, everywhere, should adopt his mantra of hope in
conjunction with peaceful co-existence.

(19) George Mitchell
– The Great Persuader

For years politicians, on both sides of the Atlantic,
Worked tirelessly, trying to persuade
Official America to adopt a more central role
In helping to solve the apparently intractable problem
Of what was, euphemistically, called
"The Troubles" in Northern Ireland.

It was only when Bill Clinton became President
That they were able to completely energise the whole process.
The new, insightful leader in the Oval office
Immediately undertook a more distinctly pro-active approach
When he selected experienced Senate chief, George Mitchell,
As a special envoy to the North.

Firstly, the latter identified the kernel of the Northern conflict.
"At the heart there is mistrust. Each disbelieves the other.
Each imagines the worst about the opposition."
Using his considerable political experience, his legal, listening
and patience skills,
The former federal judge then gradually developed a
meaningful rapport
With all the most relevant and influential political stakeholders,
both in Britain and Ireland.

By mid 1996, they were ready to accept him
As a fair, competent chairman of the negotiating team,
Entrusted with conducting complex discussions
Which would, hopefully, produce a just and lasting solution.
After two years of intense, inclusive consultations,
The consensus style, of the non-confrontational Senator
Mitchell, succeeded.

On Good Friday, 1998, all parties
Signed up to an historic accord.
A plan for devolved government was established,
A power-sharing executive proposed
And a commitment that future political decisions
Would only be agreed by peaceful, democratic means.

Six weeks later, in separate referenda,
All the people within both Irish jurisdictions endorsed the
agreement.
Today, the people of all Ireland are free
To walk and talk on the highways and in the landscapes of the
thirty two counties.
An era of mutual goodwill,
Cross - border co-operation and pragmatic patriotism
permeates the collective mindset.

Two men, from the land of our many exiles, deserve eternal
plaudits.
They had been the vital, missing pieces

In a jig saw which had puzzled so many for so long.
In the final analysis, they were responsible for convincing our local politicians
"That they were as much a part of the ultimate solution
As they were of the original problem".

And the actions of one of them - Senator George Mitchell - the great persuader,
Became the defining catalyst
For the dawning of a new and brighter future.
Countless generations of Irish people
Will be forever grateful for his magnanimous contribution
To reversing an intolerable and, seemingly, insoluble situation.

(20) Voices Of The Victims

For about thirty years, ordinary, peace-loving people
Were subjected to the daily threat of the bomb and the bullet
From paramilitaries on both sides of the sectarian divide.
Having secured an agreed political dispensation,
People on our island can now live in peace and harmony.
Still, understandably, there is a substantial residue
Of serious hurt and grievous loss felt by the relatives
And extended families of the three thousand five hundred
people who were killed.

Even though political representatives of the paramilitaries
Have verbally apologised for past acts of inhumanity,
Relatives do not like being told
"To move on, forget your personal tragedies
In the overall interest of the peace process."
As they see it, there would be no need for such a procedure
If the gunmen had not indulged
In such a nasty campaign of hatred, intimidation, bombings and
killings in the first place.

Loyalist extremists killed a thousand people,
Many of them simply because they were Catholics.
The multiple shootings of the Miami Showband members,
The assassination of the Reavey and O'Dowd families in their
own homes,
The Greysteel and Loughinisland bar deaths,

Are all stark reminders of a grim and painful past.
Bombing to death thirty three people in Monaghan and Dublin
Certainly copper-fastened their scant regard for human life in
1974.

The Provisional IRA and other Republican groups
Were responsible for the deaths of over seventeen hundred
citizens,
As they waged a vicious campaign of murder and destruction.
A work force of ten Protestant men were shot dead
When they alighted from their mini bus in Kingsmills.
A booby trap was detonated killing
Lord Mountbatten and three companions in County Sligo,
On the same day that eighteen British soldiers met a similar fate
in Warrenpoint.

Belfast's Bloody Friday and La Mon House Hotel bombings
Were particularly terrifying examples of atrocities
Carried out by the IRA.
When a massive bomb exploded at the War memorial,
In Enniskillen, killing eleven people and seriously injuring over
sixty others
There was national and worldwide condemnation on an
unprecedented scale
As there was when the Real IRA exploded a car bomb in
Omagh
Which ended the lives of twenty nine people and injured over
three hundred.

All of these horrendous incidents have deprived
The victims' relatives of a normal, enjoyable life,
Where they could share special, happy moments
Of mutual joy, births, marriages, birthdays, family celebrations.
The missing face, the absent voice, the spare chair
Will always make them reminisce of what might have been.
It is imperative that those who caused so much misery
Are, forever, conscious of contributing positively to their healing
process, their necessary and continuous rehabilitation.

Whether they be Catholic, Protestant, Irish, British, policeman,
Garda, UDR man or British soldier,
Their emotions are essentially the same.
They are sons, daughters, fathers, mothers, brothers, and sisters
of fellow human beings.
Their needs, their feelings should always take precedence
Over any political or social expediency,
To accommodate those who perpetrated such heinous crimes.
They have been our real patriots, our real heroes who suffered
and died
So that the rest of us could find true peace, true freedom.

(21) John Hume
– The Dove of Peace

In beleaguered Belfast, in 1972,
Great men of indomitable courage, of exceptional vision
Spent endless hours coherently planning
An all-inclusive New Ireland.
When you produced seven key words,
On a crumpled piece of paper, the die was cast
For a peaceful resolution of the age-old conflict
Between the Orange and the Green.

We marvelled as you stoically stood before the typist,
Passionately dictating and converting headings
Into a masterpiece of hope – a template to right all wrongs.
Totally focused, never hesitating;
You spoke sequentially, logically,
As phrases were indelibly woven
Into a brilliant, ground-breaking blueprint;
A prophetic precursor of what was to come.

For five, brief, exciting months
We dreamed your dream,
Before traditional, ingrained prejudices condemned us
Once more to another generation of suffering, of torture,
Of man's inhumanity to his fellow man;
The extremes holding us all to ransom.
But you, unceasingly, kept repeating the mantra:
"Spill sweat, not blood, unite people before territory".

For over twenty years you travelled the world
In your obsession for peace in our land.

Convincing the men of violence
That there was a better way
Was your greatest challenge, your greatest triumph,
As consultation and consensus replaced confrontation and
conflict.
Thanks to you, a troubled people
Rejoiced when our Good Friday arrived.

"The politics of the last atrocity" were over.
A quarter of a century after you signalled the way ahead
Everyone agreed to implement
What you always believed.
Even though, at times, you must have doubted
The veracity of your own thoughts
As blind hatred, the bomb and the bullet,
Constantly killed and maimed so many.

The undulating foothills
Of an ancient, monastic site stand proudly today
As the echoes of the voice of its founder – Colmcille's
"My Derry, my Derry, my little oak grove" –
Now permeate the Maiden City.
You, its tallest oak,
Making your once gerrymandered citizens happy and vibrant
Is a cameo of a whole nation at peace with itself.

John Hume – man of substance, master wordsmith,
Nobel Laureate, Champion of peace,
Take your rightful place
In the pantheon of real Irish heroes.
No one deserves it better.
No one deserves it more.

(22) The Royal Visit

In this most hallowed place
Where we remember
"All those who gave their lives
In the cause of Irish Freedom"
The English monarch took a laurel wreath
And placed it on the stand of Irish nationhood.

Impassively, respectfully, she stepped back;
Stood stoically
And bowed her head slowly, gracefully.
Not a word was uttered
Not a sound was made.
Just our nearest neighbour acknowledging our troubled history.

Yet, this significant symbolic act
Painted more than a thousand words
In the first chapter of the Book of Reconciliation
Between two neighbouring countries
Who, for many centuries, had shared
A litany of confrontation, hostility and continuous strife.

A minute's silence,
The Sounding of the Last Post,
Two heads of state
Standing together
For the first time as equals,
With a mutual respect for each other's traditions.

Both remembered the past
And what it meant,
But did not feel trapped by it
As they looked to the future.
God save Ireland.
God save Eilís a Dó, Banríon na Breataine.

Section D

A SPORTING LIFE:
Gaelic Games, Soccer and Rugby.

(23) The Terrible Twins

At the age of five, in an infants' playground,
A teaching nun first spotted two exceptionally gifted footballers.
Thanks to her imaginative coaching style,
Their inherent skills were rapidly developed and cleverly embellished.
Thus began the brilliant careers
Of the GAA's most famous footballing duo.
By early adulthood, they were Senior inter-county players,
With ever - increasing reputations for scintillating displays and outstanding performances.

For the following decade their unique combination play, their amazing artistry,
Would become legendary throughout the country.
It was, however, the All-Ireland final of 1956,
Which would set them apart in the annals of the game.
With their astute inter-passing and general brilliance,
They constantly tormented the Cork defence
To bring home Galway's first Senior title
Since the late nineteen thirties.

Sean Purcell was the creative playmaker, the guiding genius,
In the build-up to the Westerners two crucial first half goals.
Frank Stockwell was the lurking predator whose precise anticipation
Meant that, on both occasions,
The ball was instantly and accurately dispatched to the back of the net.
Purcell totally dominated the possession stakes
And never has a forward gone on such a scoring spree
As Stockwell did that September afternoon.

In the next morning's press a journalist penned the immortal
words:
"The Terrible Twins from Tuam overwhelm Cork".
And so this rhyming, lilting phrase,
Became woven into the permanent fabric of GAA folklore.
On the field of play
Each always knew what the other was gong to do.
This natural telepathy was instinctive,
Purcell's vision really incredible, Stockwell's execution
completely clinical.

Though two unassuming individuals,
They were always fulsome in their praise of each other's ability.
"Sean was so good that he could, constantly,
Make his feet do what his head dictated at any time.
He was the best all-round footballer that I ever saw."
"Frank's display in the All-Ireland final was marvellous.
To score 2-5 from play was some achievement.
All the rest of us had to do was to get the ball to him."

In the Autumn of their lives
An ongoing, chronic, arthritic condition
Confined Frank's movements outside his home.
So his old, loyal friend came to visit him, practically every day.
Sean was the quiet one, Frank the more vocal,
Different in some ways yet the same in their love of people,
their enduring friendships.
When they arrived on this earth, on the same street, within ten
days of each other,
Not one but two Terrible Beauties were born.

(24) Munich Air Disaster

During the impressionable, formative years of our Primary and
Secondary school days,
We are considerably influenced
By the people we see, the events that occur, the deeds that are
done.
A serious air crash, one February afternoon in 1958,
Confirmed, crystallised that philosophy for me.
Just before I walked the half-mile to school on the following
morning
I was, as usual, casually listening to the news on the radio.
Only this time the tenor, the substance, the solemnity of the
newscaster's voice, suddenly attracted my undivided attention.

An aeroplane carrying home the Manchester United soccer
team
And a group of journalists from an European cup-tie
Had crashed, after failing to take-off properly in the icy, snowy
conditions at Munich airport.
After hearing the names of the seven players, amongst others,
that were immediately killed, I rushed off to school.
I now realised, for the first time, the extremely thin line that
existed between mortality and immortality, between life and
death
And how a famous soccer team that included
International stars like Tommy Taylor, Roger Byrne and Liam
Whelan
Could, without any warning, be instantly, completely wiped out.

Shortly after my arrival, the young male teacher from the classroom next door, ashen-faced, clearly deeply disturbed, dashed into our room.
"Does anyone know the names of the Manchester United players who were killed yesterday?" he plaintively beseeched.
Nowadays that type of question would reflect the normal kind of interaction between teacher and pupil.
But back then that was not the case.
So I hesitated, before taking a deep breath, and repeated ad verbatim what I had heard.
As I called out each name, his face grew longer, his voice dropped several octaves,
Until he eventually just stood there, staring absent-mindedly into space,
whispering what a brilliant footballing team they were.
Obviously a loyal soccer follower, ahead of his time in our locality, his speech became barely audible as he thanked me for having such a good memory.

Gradually, the whole media hype surrounding the Munich tragedy
Increased immensely the profile of soccer on a global basis.
Out of this unprecedented awareness, along with millions of others,
I found an immediate outlet to develop an inherent interest
In a sport that transcended colour, race, creed, national boundaries.
We could, we can, discuss anywhere, at any time,
The common language of a game that has produced outstanding contests of impeccable skill,
players of unquestionable talent
Whilst still retaining our national identity, our own cultural, indigenous sporting pursuits.

A proverbial plethora of ingenious, skilful performers have
adorned the game.
Connoisseurs have always treasured the positional play of the
elegant Bobby Moore,
the sheer class of the multi-gifted Franz Beckenbauer,
The incisive, creative wizardry of Best, Pele, Cruyff, Maradona
and Messi, amongst so many others,
Who have contributed tremendously to the universal popularity
of the sport.
Master Dargan certainly had the intelligence, the broad-
mindedness,
Back in that classroom to appreciate true greatness
From wherever it emanated.
He really was a man ahead of his time.

(25) A Nation Once Again

The eight hundred year-old history between Ireland and England
Is a perfect reflection of the distinctly uneasy relationship
That normally exists between a conqueror and the conquered,
Always fluctuating from the tolerant to the intolerant, from the
cruel to the discriminatory.
On one November Sunday, in 1920, it reached an all-time low,
Beginning with the IRA's cold – blooded assassination of thirteen
British undercover agents in their beds
And ending with the English killing three IRA suspects in Dublin
castle.
However, that first Bloody Sunday is best remembered for the
unprovoked brutality that occurred in between.

Five thousand spectators were happily watching a Gaelic football
match, in Croke Park, between Tipperary and Dublin,
When British security forces suddenly surrounded the perimeter of
the venue.
They, indiscriminately, fired numerous shots into the crowd,
Shooting dead fourteen innocent civilians, including Tipperary
player, Michael Hogan.
Thereafter, Croke Park became, in the eyes of many, a permanent
shrine to Irish Nationalism,
A place in common with all Gaelic grounds, where the GAA's
Rule 42
Did not permit the playing of English games such as Soccer, Rugby
or Cricket.
Indeed over eighty years later, at the turn of the twenty first
century, this contentious rule was still in situ, still adhered to.

In the early 2000s it was decided to redevelop Lansdowne Road,
The home venue for Ireland's international soccer and rugby sides,
into a modern stadium.
As the ground would be closed for the development process
Both organisations would be forced to play their home matches
abroad.
Rather than seeing their fellow sportsmen and spectators being
subjected to such expense and inconvenience,
Many GAA followers, including new President, Sean Kelly,
Felt that Rule 42 should be modified to accommodate
The playing of international soccer and rugby games, in Croke
Park, in the interim.

Because of the foresight, courage and diplomatic skills of Kelly
And the widespread support amongst the ordinary members,
the GAA, at its annual Congress, acceded to the temporary change
of the rule.
Nevertheless, there was a residue of bitterness, of rancour,
Amongst some of the Association's more conservative membership,
among the more extreme Nationalists
Who contended that the adoption of such an agreement was an act
of betrayal
To those who died, in 1920, and subsequently, at the behest of
British forces.
The real, acid test for the successful implementation of the new
ruling
Would be the international rugby game between England and
Ireland, in Croke Park, in February 2007.

Over eighty two thousand people packed the stadium when that
day of destiny arrived.
As the English side ran out into the famous arena
They got a magnificent reception from everyone.

When the Irish team emerged the noise was deafening in its
intensity, overwhelming in its expectation.
Then came the moment to await what had never happened before
in the cathedral of the GAA,
The singing of the English national anthem, "God save the
Queen".
From the Irish spectators came not one iota of negativity,
Just the utmost regard, due respect that one would expect from
good neighbours, close friends.

The proudest moment of all was when the band struck up Amhrán
na bhFiann.
Never was any anthem, anywhere sung with such gusto, such
feeling.
Watching front row stalwarts, Jerry Flannery and John Hayes,
With tears streaming down their faces, was an amazing sight
As they intimately embraced the hand and heart of eight centuries
of hostile history.
Thanks to the strong, inspiring leadership of one man
The GAA were no longer prisoners of their understandable past
But powerful, positive brokers for peace, harmony and the only
unity that really matters- the unity of people.

What made the whole scenario of euphoria more fulfilling
Was the fact that Ireland played superbly to record a terrific victory.
The impeccable markmanship of outhalf, Ronan O'Gara
And the three great tries stand out as a pertinent cameo
Of a really fantastic triumph.
Winger, Shane Horgan's try was particularly appropriate.
His brilliant Gaelic-type overhead catch before diving over for an
opportunist try
Really exemplified that each code, both on and off the field, could
unite to make Ireland a real nation once again.

(26) Two Hurling Aristocrats
– Christy Ring and Henry Shefflin

It was the day that one of the game's greatest-ever hurlers
Played his last full Railway Cup match in Croke Park.
Forty two year-old Christy Ring was in the dying twilight of a star-studded career.
For fifty five minutes the Cork and Cloyne maestro was relatively quiet.
Suddenly, he literally took off, halfway between the fourteen yards line and the parallelogram.
His whole body was uniformly suspended in mid-air, three feet from the ground, parallel to it.
With perfect split-second anticipation, he extended his hurley just as the sliotar sped towards the right hand side of the square.
With a deft, synchronised twist of wrists, of hands, he connected with the ball
And sent an incredible, reverse, angular shot, unexpectedly, unerringly, towards the left corner of the Leinster net.
That was the final farewell and glorious, provincial reprise of a hurling genius.

On that St Patrick's Day, I saw my first competitive hurling match.
Seeing Ring and all the others, in the flesh, display such exceptional skill, made me a lifetime fan of our national game.
To me there is no greater spectacle in the sporting world.
There is no better or more enthralling sight than to see a defender or midfielder
Rise majestically, high in the air, to pluck a ball with his hand, from amongst a mini-forest of clashing hurleys
And then come down and sidestep all opponents before sending a long, relieving clearance downfield.

To watch a dashing forward with the sliotar apparently glued to
the caman, magically weaving his way through a packed defence,
Before striking, off either his right or left hand side, is another
wondrous art form.
To observe the bravery, the anticipatory skills of the game's most
talented goalkeepers
Instantly, spontaneously, arching their reflex movements to dart
across a crowded goalmouth,
To affect a breath-taking save is one of the most singularly
fantastic feats in any sport.
Unique skills like overhead striking, rolling lifts and ground
striking, completely enhance the totality of this beautiful, graceful
game.

Since that swan song of the irrepressible Ring, I have watched
eight different counties
Impressively lay claim to the coveted Liam MacCarthy Cup on
All-Ireland Final Day.
There have been many stupendous performances of pure class,
sheer, unadulterated artistry.
But none to compare with the consistently high standards
That Kilkenny's Henry Shefflin has attained during the first
decade of the new millennium.
His mastery of all the skills: his phenomenal work rate: his
exemplary team play
Have been an inspiring microcosm of absolute brilliance.
He has won every honour, at every level, for club, county,
province.
He has broken all records, including being the top all-time scorer
in championship hurling;
The first GAA player in either code to receive ten All-Star Awards.
Not only is he the most outstanding player of his generation,
King Henry, undoubtedly, is one of the greatest players of all time.

(27) Magical Memories Of A September Sunday

Sitting in the study hall
Of an old, grey college building,
Spending a lonely, boarding school Sunday afternoon,
Listening to the golden voice emanating
From a battered, brown radio in the corner;
Our minds wandered back in time
As our thoughts dovetailed perfectly
Into feelings of isolation and hopelessness.

For years we had felt disillusioned,
Almost totally abandoned,
Though patronised by some with
"You are great for keeping the GAA alive."
Yet we knew there was no real ambition,
No chance of progress or success;
Just loosely, attached antennae
On the periphery of where we wanted to be

Our games were really for the Kerrys and Kilkennys,
The Corks and Dublins of this world.
Sometimes the Louths, Roscommons, Waterfords and Armaghs,
Would suddenly appear on the horizon,
Only to disappear rapidly into the abyss
Where the rest of us permanently resided;
Often eliminated in the first round,
Rarely going any further than the second.

Along came a man of clear vision,
A person of definite purpose, of real substance.
Different structures were laid, visionary strategies planned,
And the best footballers in the Mournes
Perfectly positioned.
The ethic of team play, on and off the field,
Became paramount;
Everyone singularly focused on the same, specific goal.

That day of days, that moment of truth, had now arrived.
The footballers of Down were ready
For whatever was placed in front of them.
Running out to an almighty roar
And a huge unfurling of the red and black,
Kevin Mussen led his warriors
To the cauldron of their destiny;
Kerry in their twenty ninth - Down in their first.

The first half ebbed and flowed
As first David and then Goliath exchanged leading roles,
Before the short whistle sounded.
With the Northern stars in front by two
At half time, the excitement was palpable, almost unbearable,
As that dream of dreams became more attainable
For every man, woman and child
Who had travelled southwards from early morn.

In the second half a long James McCartan lob
Was the defining catalyst for each Down player
To be released from the shackles of history and mediocrity.
When a Paddy Doherty penalty special put them six ahead,
The whole arena spontaneously erupted
Into a cacophony of joy and anticipated glory.
Kerry supporters stunned into silence;
Down fans praying for the remaining minutes to pass quickly
and easily.

They need not have worried.
The Mourne work rate increased immensely.
New heights of skill were scaled.
The full repertoire of their collective artistry
Was displayed with exquisite panache and exhilarating beauty.
The Ballykinlar bricklayer, in particular,
Nonchalantly executing unprecedented levels of scoring
excellence;
To seal a momentous occasion.

When the final whistle sounded
Down had not just won a marvellous football match,
They had captured the hearts of a national and admiring
audience.
Down were the All-Ireland football champions,
The voice on the radio said.
A great football team had accomplished
What others ignored.
We really were a nation once again.

Leaving the study hall excited, exuberant;
Momentarily forgetting the chores of books and learning
And the boring repetition of a secondary school routine,
A freshly-found freedom occupied our minds;
People of similarity, of aspiration,
With realistic hopes for a future of distinction.
Those magical words, "Down are 1960 All-Ireland football champions",
Eliminated the insecurities of the past and fostered togetherness for the future.

To Kevin Mussen and his side of heroes;
We say, no team anywhere will ever surpass
What you did for us.
More emphatically-you were the best because you were first
To remove the iron curtain of suspicion and division,
And bring supporter-friendly, player-friendly Gaelic football
Across the four provinces of Ireland
And to future generations of all our people.

And Maurice Hayes we are glad
That you "Let Go Your Anchor"
On Sweet Killough Bay!
And opened your heart and mind
To a better way of doing things
For the Gaelic footballers of Down and, by extension, every other county.
With you calculated planning and prophetic perception
You have become the real Star of the County Down.

(28) Harry Gregg – An Irish Hero

As the plane attempted to take-off, for the third time,
There was a deafening silence, a palpable fear amongst the
passengers.
A tall, young Derry goalkeeper
Who had joined the Busby Babes, just two months previously,
was particularly nervous.
Thinking of the dreadful probability of an ominous, unfolding
scenario,
His fellow Irishman, the supremely talented, inside forward
Liam Whelan,
Tried to pacify his custodian with a beaming smile, a silent
prayer, and a succinct sentence.
"Harry, if it is going to happen, I'm ready for it."

Those were the last words that Harry Gregg remembers
From that fated aircraft which, moments later, plunged
powerfully, sideways, before crashing heavily
Onto the periphery of the treacherous, snow-laden runway,
Killing over twenty people, seriously injuring many others.
Momentarily, he thought he was dead,
And he felt grateful for having had a good life, a happy family.
But then, suddenly, he realised within the despairing, interior
darkness that he was alive, miraculously uninjured.
Seeing a shaft of light he crawled through a hole in the fuselage
and scrambled his way outside.

Ignoring the pleading of the pilot not to return inside the
stricken plane,
He immediately set himself the courageous, almost impossible
task of rescuing as many people as he could.
For the next quarter of an hour he worked frantically,
unselflessly, fearlessly,
To save other passengers from impending death when the plane
would, inevitably, explode.
Having entered the dismembered bowels of the smouldering
wreckage,
He found, first of all, a young child beneath a pile of debris,
anxiously crying.
He carried her to the safety of the gaping, fuselage exit,
Before returning down the plane to lift her pregnant mother,
pushing both of them outside into the waiting arms of other
rescuers.

At the back of the plane, he found
The still figures of his playing colleagues, Bobby Charlton,
Denis Viollet, their bodies hanging, half in, half out.
Presuming they were dead, he dragged them into seats that had
been flung from the wreckage.
With the tail of the plane now ablaze, he noticed, amongst
the devastation, his seriously injured manager, Matt Busby,
stabilised him, propped him up in a seat away from danger.
Next he discovered his old school friend, now playing colleague,
Jackie Blanchflower.
Watching him crying bitterly, with his arm bleeding profusely
And their esteemed captain Roger, Byrne, lying across him,
dead,
Was an especially poignant, heart-breaking moment.

Having tied a tourniquet, with his tie, around Jackie's arm
Harry now knew nothing more could be done, especially with a
series of loud explosions turning the whole scene into a burning
inferno.
Amidst the cauldron of despair, of tragedy, one item of good
news
Was to suddenly see Bobby and Denis standing alive and well,
staring into the fires' raging flames.
So relieved was he to see them and other passengers safe and
sound,
That he sank to his knees, in the cold, miserable slush, and
thanked God.
Later that year, Harry was selected as the best goalkeeper in the
world
For his magnificent displays with Northern Ireland in the World
Cup finals in Sweden.

In subsequent years, Zoran Lukic, the unborn, Yugoslav child
whom Harry had, unknowingly, rescued
Often heard his now elderly mother recalling
The heroic deeds of an Irish goalkeeper on that awful day back
in 1958.
He had spent his whole life yearning to thank him personally,
For ensuring three members of his family, including himself,
Were bravely saved from the premature finality of a terrible
death
And were each given the gift of an enjoyable, meaningful life.
But, strict Communist laws had, for years, prevented him from
any association with Westerners.

However, in 2008, those types of restrictions had been removed
And 49-year-old Zoran, in his own house in Belgrade, met
Harry for the first time.
They chatted for endless hours about their respective lives
And shed many tears of joy, of sorrow.
Harry Gregg had made numerous, spectacular, footballing saves
In the world's leading soccer stadia.
But, unquestionably, that seventh, unknown human save in a
far-off German airfield,
Was his greatest and most rewarding save of all.

(29) Boyhood Dream

Ever since I first heard the golden voice
Of that creator of picturesque, sporting scenarios,
That commentator extraordinary, the inimitable Michael
O'Hehir,
The only place that I wanted to be
Was in the cathedral of Gaelic Games that is Croke Park
And to see my native county not only compete
But win the Sam Maguire Cup
On All-Ireland football final day.

All my family, friends, neighbours, along with thousands of like-
minded supporters
From every club and parish in the county would be there,
For a day of unprecedented, communal enjoyment and glorious
celebration.
The pre-match build-up would be intense, all – embracing,
enthralling,
As our whole county would band together to become an
integral part of the national consciousness,
And the local names of previously little, unknown places
Would resonate, loudly, movingly,
Across the many different airwaves, indeed across the world.

For a few magical weeks, our county
Would be the magnetic focal point of the country's curiosity.
Older and forgotten heroes who had often honoured the oak
leaf symbol,
For county and province, in less exalted times,

Would suddenly be resurrected
From the dusty archives of partially fulfilled experiences of
success.
They would now take their rightful place
Amongst our new exponents of football creativity, our future
celebrities for years to come.

After many false dawns, numerous hard luck stories,
The great day actually arrived.
We waited expectantly, though anxiously, and with bated breath
As the long hour of our destiny duly came;
Standing to attention, facing the tricolour,
Just like the ace commentator had often said,
We stood solemnly, respectfully, listened with total intent
When the Artane Boys' Band belted out Amhrán na bhFiann.

We looked lovingly, yet apprehensively, at each other.
Then, cursorily, glanced across the vast arena,
Seeing everywhere, men, women, children from our heartlands,
Places like Dungiven, Swatragh, Ballinascreen, Glenullin,
Lavey;
Magherafelt, Maghera, Bellaghy, Ballinderry and our own
Lissan home.
People, who from early childhood, had travelled many miles and
suffered much
In their pursuit of one solitary objective.
This was their hour, their moment of truth.

The ball was thrown in,

There was no going back now.

Prayers were said. Posterity awaited

As fifteen neatly-clad Derry men had the signal honour,

But the mighty task, some said insurmountable,

Of delivering a county's cumulative years

Of heavenly expectation, of eternal hope, within their minds,

their hearts,

But most of all through their gifted hands, their skilful feet.

After seventy minutes of sheer intensity, unbearable excitement,

Moments of despair, temporary ecstasy,

The end drew near

With Derry, nervously, leading by three points.

Bombarding their defence,

Like a siege from far-off historical times,

Cork made one last desperate effort to snatch an equalising

goal.

But the northern defence, resolutely, stood firm.

Then from amongst a crowded parallelogram,

Emerged our prolific marksman, with the most cultured of left

feet.

Enda Gormley had the ball securely in hand.

Simultaneously, the referee blew the full-time whistle.

It was 4.57pm on September 19[th,] 1993.

In unison, Enda and the precious pigskin rose high in the air;

The first public, physical acknowledgment,

Of a famous victory had just occurred.

Twenty thousand Derry supporters burst out of the stands, the
terraces,
Shouting, screaming exclamations of delight,
Bearing smiles of total happiness, shedding tears of pure joy,
Before enveloping the expansive, green sward.
In a seething sea of red and white;
And Enda Gormley, in his hour of triumph,
Did not forget an incapacitated former footballing star, his
uncle, Colm P.
As he immediately rushed over to embrace him in the
wheelchair spectator section.

When Henry Downey raised aloft the Sam Maguire Cup,
A lifetime of hard luck stories, acute disappointments, were at
an end.
My childhood dream had become a magnificent, living reality
And I was privileged to be able to share
In such a fantastic occasion for my homeland;
An honour denied to so many, other worthy recipients;
At long last we had taken our place in the pantheon of great
teams.
Derry really were All-Ireland football champions.

(30) Farewell, Dear Cormac

In the land of O'Neill, the meandering Blackwater flows,
As it did in the time of Hugh and Owen Roe.
Between embattled Benburb and historic Dungannon
Lies Eglish, a haven of rural tranquillity,
Where you first saw the light of day,
Just twenty four years ago.

In Derrylatinee, the always pensive, enquiring, scholarly mind,
With the smiling, friendly personality,
Developed rapidly and effortlessly progressed.
When you arrived at the See of St Patrick,
On Armagh's hallowed, sandy hill, a long, ingrained tradition
Of MacRory excellence awaited you.

Those twin characteristics of that ancient seat of classical
learning
Were greatly enhanced with your penchant for the game of the
Gael,
And the constant thirst for all-embracing knowledge,
Captaining SPCA to All-Ireland Quiz success
Was the first public leadership role of the budding man
We would come to love and admire.

Luck twice deserted you in 1997;
Losing Paul to a freak of nature and your minor team going
down
In your theatre of dreams, deeply hurt.
Recording a treble triumph in the following years
As you lifted Tom Markham and Tadgh O Cléirigh,
Heralded you as the best young footballer in the land.

Wearing No 3 was the catalyst
For inscribing Tír Eoghain on Gaeldom's greatest prize.
In a continuous cavalcade of euphoric, unbridled emotion,
You traversed a county starved of success, celebrating its
greatest achievement.
Returning to Eglish, with me, you had become Brantry's pride
and joy;
Its most famous son, its most unassuming hero.

2004 looked ideal for a good team to become great.
Being handed the new baton,
Made your sense of destiny almost inevitable.
But Divine intervention dictated that when
You raised up the McKenna Cup to a Donegal sky
You would never again adorn the playing fields of Ireland.

The gracious graduate of Queen's and UCD,
The wonderful teacher at St Catherine's was now no more.
A leader, a talismanic figure; surely an embryonic statesman;
A person of loyalty, substance, spirituality, suddenly left us in
our greatest hour.
So hard to understand, so easy to remember
"Why God's ways are not our ways".

Never in the history of our island
Has any human being, so young in years,
Yet so mature in temperament, made such a national, indelible
impact.
That winning, laughing aura of confidence,
Though humble acquiescence, enveloped a people
So desperate for real icons of transparent humanity.

For years your people craved for me to come
Amongst you and I did.
Those last, earthly days of yours, I was especially privileged
To be at the epicentre of a nation,
Saying goodbye to a football prince
Whose deeds will inspire countless generations to come.

Still, hope springs eternal,
As my alter ego, the original of the species, tells me.
When you arrived beyond heaven's door
You immediately sought a team meeting
With all the other GAA greats, cut down in the prime of life,
So suddenly, so, apparently, unfairly.

Gallant John Joe, P.J. of Stradone, Pat of Coolderry
Are but a sample few who answered the latest call
Of Cormac, a true High King, to one and all.
"Always help those down below to cope
With the sheer fragility of life
And the ultimate reality of death".

Farewell, Dear Cormac, you have served
Your family, parish, county and country well.
When our time comes, *le cúnamh Dé*, we will see you again
At the eternal game up in the sky.
Your nearest and dearest, as before, will once more walk and
talk with you,
Only this time - it will be forever.

(31) The Golden Generation

One of the most powerful impulses of my childhood curiosity
Was to learn all about the diverse sports that were broadcast on
the radio.
The annual rugby international series was one such competition
Which commanded my instant, enthusiastic attention.
The vivid, accurate portrayals of the game and its players, by an
assortment of commentators,
Allowed me to understand, to visualise the complexities of a
new sporting language.
Incorporating the repetitive procedures of scrums, rucks, mauls,
line-outs,
The titles of the various positions and the functions of each of
the fifteen participants.

It was, however, my inherent desire to have a personal hero, a
national side with which to identity,
That really attracted, enthused me.
The elusive body swerves, the phenomenal pace, the accurate
kicking
Of that magnificent out half, Jack Kyle,
Transformed me every time I "watched him!"
But I waited, in vain, for he and his teammates
To replicate the heroics of a Grand Slam and successive Triple
crowns
That Ireland and Jack had accomplished in the previous decade.

For the next thirty years Ireland had many talented, even world-
class individuals,
Like the tall, pacy winger, Tony O'Reilly who performed many

try - scoring records on two Lions tours,
The irrepressible, magical genius that was the versatile centre,
Mike Gibson,
The legendary, five-time Lions' tourist and second row par
excellence, Willie John McBride.
But, unfortunately, they were not on teams of sufficient quality,
power or finesse
To land the now elusive Triple crown, the dream prize of every
rugby player on these islands.
It would be the 1980's before such success
Would again lift the spirits of an expectant nation.

In 1982, prop Gerry "Ginger" McLoughlin scored one of
rugby's greatest-ever tries
When he carried half of the Irish pack with him before he
touched down,
In a narrow but deserved win over "the auld enemy."
Out half, Ollie Campbell, with some electrifying breaks,
Scored all of Ireland's twenty one points when they outclassed
Scotland
To secure their first Triple crown in thirty three years.
Three years later, the Irish replicated this feat, in spectacular
fashion,
With a sensational last-minute drop goal, by Michael Kiernan,
to snatch a three-point victory over England.

There was another barren period until the "Golden
Generation" came along in the 2000's.
Three Triple crowns were impressively accumulated in 2004,
2006, and 2007.
Ireland now had an unequalled amount of outstanding players.
Centres, Brian O'Driscoll and Gordon D'Arcy were terrific backs.

O'Driscoll was, arguably, one of the best players ever to don an Irish jersey.

Half backs, Ronan O'Gara and Peter Stringer were a brilliant combination; O'Gara a supreme line and place kicker.

Paul O'Connell and Donncha O'Callaghan were powerful men in the second row; O'Connell a real, talismanic figure.

Yet, despite their individual and collective abilities, the Grand Slam always eluded them.

As the 2009 season began everyone knew, though no one would say it,

That if it ever was going to happen this would be the year of the Holy Grail.

Excellent tries by Jamie Heaslip and O'Driscoll plus superb kicking by O'Gara,

Enabled the Irish to overcome the French in the first game,

Before comfortably defeating the Italians in the next.

A close, hard-fought victory over England,

Followed by an impressive seven-point win against Scotland, in Murrayfield,

Meant all Ireland waited, in joyful expectation, for the Grand Slam decider against Wales in Cardiff.

Two spectacular tries, within two second-half minutes; set Irish pulses racing.

First, the immaculate O'Driscoll sneaked away from the side of a ruck to touch down.

Next, following a delicate chip ahead by O'Gara, winger, Tommy Bowe cleverly sped through the Welsh cover for an opportunist score under the posts.

However, with only five minutes left, Ireland trailed the Dragons by a point.

But, with two and a half minutes remaining, the ever-reliable
O'Gara dropped a goal to put the visitors ahead by two.
As the clock nervously edged towards the eightieth and last
minute,
An Irish transgression gave the Welsh a penalty, forty eight
metres from the Irish posts.
Stephen Jones' well-directed kick appeared to be on its winning
way but tantalisingly, veered left and wide in the last ten metres
of its trajectory.

Immediately, the full time whistle sounded.
All the anguish, the bitter disappointments of the past, were lost
in the euphoria of the present.
Captain, Brian O'Driscoll and his fellow heroes deserved
the spontaneous acclamation of all Irish people at home and
abroad.
As I watched the closing television sequence of pictures,
A youthful eighty three year old John Wilson Kyle, smiled
serenely in the stand.
Ironically, it was the first time I had seen him "live at a rugby
match!"
After sixty years of yearning, of hope, he said that he could not
be happier.
Thus the mantle of the achievements of this most gracious of
great players had, at last, been passed onto an exceptionally
worthy group of successors.

(32) Colm Cooper
– A Footballing Artist

Deft of foot and sleight of hand,
He glides effortlessly across Gaelic football's many green
pastures,
As if defenders did not exist, as if out for a casual morning stroll.
Suddenly, the razor-sharp intuitive footballing brain
Clicks into overdrive, momentarily weighing up his options,
To pass, to shoot, to go right, to go left or none of these.
Almost instantaneously the mind answers and
He lofts the ball beautifully, nonchalantly, over the bar with
either foot,
Or clinically dispatches the accelerating leather,
With equal aplomb and deadly accuracy to the corner of the net.

An immaculate first touch, regardless of the angle or the height,
Totally in command, just sheer poetry in motion.
The ball appears to be a magnetic extension
Of varied limb and body movements.
Infinitely flexible, always perfectly co-ordinated.
Though a brilliant individual,
He inevitably orchestrates what is best for the team,
Invariably turning, twisting to allow his remarkable radar –
vision
Execute a probing defence – splitting pass
Or avoid a would-be desperate tackle.

The vast repertoire of his silken, uncanny skills,
Electrify friend and adversary alike.
Making them marvel at a true sporting genius.
No matter how great the occasion,
No matter how formidable an opponent,
He makes the extraordinary look elementary,
The ordinary something delightful to behold.
With consummate ease he wriggles free from impossibly tight
defensive situations,
To display his unique dexterity in how to create havoc
And leave frustrated backs trailing in his wake.

A century ago another wonderful Kerry footballer,
Another Dr Crokes' special talent,
Strode the GAA scene as a talismanic forward.
Dick Fitzgerald, a double All-Ireland winning captain,
Was the author of "How to play Gaelic football."
Today, another Killarney protégé, Colm Cooper,
Has put "Dickeens" theory into practice
To an incredible degree of proficiency and ingenuity.
Undoubtedly, the ginger-haired, baby-faced star
Is the greatest forward of his generation.

Section E

PERSONAL FAVOURITES:

People who made a Difference.
Spiritual Reflections.

(33) Lough Patrick

Just off the main road between Draperstown and Cookstown,
Lies an oval-shaped mountain lake, an oasis of tranquillity, and
a haven of peace.
An acre and a half of calm, clear, undiluted water
Is bounded by almost seventy acres of rare, rich flora and
numerous species of indigenous, wild life.
Clothed in purple and crimson heather,
It is an untouched landscape of natural, scenic beauty,
Amidst a rambling countryside of ancient, archaeological
artefacts;
Druid circles, unique burial chambers.

Steeped in traditional folklore, its most famous anecdote recalls
St Patrick.
Around the lake's perimeter reclines a downtrodden path
Which encapsulates centuries of pilgrims' footprints, of visitors'
curiosity.
Legend has it that Patrick and a group of his faithful followers,
Held a prayer station here in the townland of Owenreagh,
In the historic parish of Ballinascreen.
After a tough day's hiking and many hours of meditation,
They became thirsty but could not find any water to drink.

Seeing their predicament, the Patron saint pulled up a rush
from the blanket bogland.
Immediately, powerfully, water noisily gushed forth in torrents,

Bequeathing to posterity the splendid, hollowed lake that exists today.
After this miraculous occurrence the whole area became associated with prayer, penance, cures.
A century later Derry's own saint – Colmcille – went on a pilgrimage to this now holy place.
So impressed was he with its serenity, its suitability as a centre of spiritual retreat,
He decided that, in future years,
A three-day annual mission should begin on St John's Eve to celebrate the sacred spot.

For the following fifteen hundred years, the people from not only Derry, but also Tyrone
And across the entire northern half of Ireland,
Came on those mid-summer days to pray for peace of mind,
To seek cures for their illnesses, their physical ailments.
At the same time, in later years, the rest of the neighbouring populace,
Throughout the adjacent hills, the valleys of the Sperrins,
Prayed for blessings for their crops, freedom from disease,
As they danced, sang and played music to the background of blazing fires on what was known as Bonfire night, in the month of June.

Each prayer station consisted of every pilgrim walking barefooted,
Three times around the lake while praying
And then nine times, on their knees, around a nearby tummock.

To fully complete the ritual,
Those people seeking cures were then dipped in the water.
Before departing they left behind a lock of their hair or an item
of clothing.
It was said that this symbolic gesture
Signalled the illness, disease or worry leaving the affected
person.

Most unofficial religious shrines, such as Lough Patrick,
Have a record of some uncertainty, occasional controversy, even
conflict,
Between what is considered a representation of official church
teaching
And what is perceived as a superstitious reincarnation of pagan
observances.
Regardless of these contrasting philosophies,
Lough Patrick intrinsically develops a suitable ambience for
prayerful meditation at a place, at a pace,
Which recreates the same environment in which people like
Patrick and Comcille did so much,
To spread the true message of Christianity in the first place.

(34) Twelve Minutes To Midnight

Having arrived in the O'Farrell county town, my brother and I
headed for the nearest restaurant.
The proprietor was a friendly, talkative individual with an
encyclopaedic knowledge of the GAA.
He told us, if we wanted a real secure life, we should settle in
Longford and join his local football club - the greatest in Ireland!
When we asked him where was the best, the nearest dancing
venue,
He immediately referred us to a Carnival dance that night, in a
place called Ballinalee,
A village, some ten miles away, which once had a very famous
blacksmith.

Thanks to our newfound tour guide, we soon arrived at his
selected, musical mecca.
There was a huge crowd that had come to see a local showband
star make his debut on home territory.
As the night evolved, we were happily relaxed with no
extraordinary expectations.
That feeling, however, changed suddenly when I spotted a dark-
haired girl dancing in perfect rhythm to the beat of the band.
She had a singularly engaging smile, a neatly, attractively formed
dimple on one cheek.
Gradually I began to think, "Maybe tonight would not be so
ordinary after all."

We met at twelve minutes to midnight.
The die was now cast and her ability to converse, effortlessly,
across the varied spectra

Of music, literature, politics and the GAA was captivating;
indeed very impressive,
Especially, considering that it was all done
Within the limitations of a twelve-minute, three-dance sequence.
The broad range of interests excitedly complimented the
outward good looks; the ever pleasant, happy appearance.

Four years later we, joyfully, walked down the aisle as husband
and wife.
The unique, Spanish architectural design of Clonbroney church
And a gloriously sunny day
Were the magically, magnificent backdrops to the radiance of the
girl on my arm.
Ever since, she has been my listening ear, my constant
conscience, my steadfast rock.
But, most of all, she is the caring, capable mother of our now two
grown-up children.

They, in turn, whilst retaining their individual, endearing
characteristics, their distinctive interests,
Have always replicated our core values of loyalty, trust, caring,
family integrity.
Every so often I meet that prophetic restaurateur who directed
me to that marquee dance so many years ago.
Like the rest of us, he is older and wiser now but still friendly,
still talkative.
Incidentally, he still maintains Longford Slashers are the best
club in Ireland.
Maybe he is right!

(35) Seamus Heaney's Literary Debut

Life at St Joseph's Teacher Training College was a totally
fulfilling, immensely enjoyable experience,
Where all of us had a tremendous sense of mutual trust, close
friendship, deep loyalty,
Not only with our fellow students but more interestingly with
the lecturing and administrative staffs as well.
The contrast between this integrated third level involvement
And the various participants in our respective secondary
schools
Could not have been starker, more different.
Gone was the dogmatic, though sometimes necessary,
demarcation limits, the seemingly endless formalities of
officialdom,
The rigid application of Rule Book dictates and the daily
checklists of dos and don'ts.
Meaningful dialogue, amiable engaging conversations and an
all-embracing camaraderie
Were most welcome replacements, the outstanding hallmarks of
life back at "The Ranch".

At second level we were always very conscious of which year we
were in.
Established practice, amongst some students, dictated that the
longer we were there, the more important we were.
And conversely, the younger, in years, the less worthy,
The more nondescript in the greater scheme of things.
The traditional pecking order, the superiority of seniority,
Led to infrequent intimidation, even subconscious bullying, by
a tiny minority of the more dominant personalities.
Unfortunately, this tended to make life, school life - especially

for boarders - somewhat miserable, quite unpalatable for the more vulnerable.
And unfairly tarnished the vast majority who were always decent and fair to everyone.
But at St Joseph's, regardless of age, year or status, equality, respect,
Were the ever-present, and always applied tenets of the college's mission principles.

For the three years of the course we had a marvellous time socially,
Dancing to dozens of showbands in every venue within reach, within reason, several times a week.
One famous weekend, two particularly adventuresome dance fans
Went, on three successive nights, to Banbridge, Dublin, Cork.
Having travelled a round trip of over four hundred miles,
They were, unbelievably, back in the college by Monday afternoon.
Despite the intensity of our varied entertainment activities,
We did find time to attend lectures regularly, study reasonably hard, and prepare properly for teaching practice.
However, during that time, what at first seemed ordinary enough, in hindsight became
The most extraordinary defining moment in all of our time at Trench House.

One afternoon our young English lecturer, as unpretentious, as genial as ever,
Walked into the lecture hall, armed with his usual, self-effacing smile and a big box of books.
"Folks, I have written a few poems which have been put together

Into a book called "Death of a Naturalist."
I thought I would give you a copy each.
You are the first group to get one. I hope you like it."
So said future Nobel literature prizewinner and world-
renowned poet, Seamus Heaney.
As a proud member of one of his first third level classes I still
feel privileged and honoured to have been present
On one of the most historic occasions in Irish Literature,
The official literary birth of a Nobel Prize winner.

Over four decades later, on a bright August morning, the
shattering news filtered through.
A stunned nation, the disbelieving world of literature,
But most of all, his devoted wife Marie and their three grown-
up children,
Could not believe that such a wonderfully loving, friendly,
family man had left them so unexpectedly.
The bouncy, physical presence, the heart-warming countenance
was gone forever.
But his magnanimous spirit, his powerful scholastic legacy,
The countless, memorably resonating phrases
Which he so cleverly, seamlessly, embroidered
Into a beautiful patchwork quilt of poetic elegance,
Will be eternally ingrained in the consciousness of all of us for
years to come.

For the last time Seamus Heaney slowly, carefully, journeyed
northwards.
Crossing the Bann from Antrim to Derry at Toomebridge
Had distinct echoes of an historic impasse when impending
confrontation had denied easier access.
Travelling down the Toome Road and passing many of the

places so inextricably linked with many of his greatest writings
Was a particularly poignant reminder of how a great poet
Made the local global and Derry fondly recalled, wherever and
whenever the literati read and learned.
Toner's Bog where his father cut more turf than any other man:
Mossbawn where he first saw the light of day.
Anahorish whose most, famous past pupil will be eternally
remembered and revered.
Turning right at Hillhead,
his former GAA club, St Malachy's Castledawson
Saluted an old stalwart, the nephew of their famed talisman,
the one and only Sonny McCann.

Now he was just a few miles from his final resting place.
As he reached Bellaghy, thousands of his friends from near and
far had gathered to say goodbye.
A lone piper serenaded the cortege up from The Diamond on
the remaining stretch to St Mary's Churchyard.
The Primary schoolchildren of his first Alma Mater led him to
the graveside.
The packed cemetery was completely hushed in their respect,
totally focused on the arrival of their special friend.
In a simple, moving eulogy Fr Andy Dolan welcomed back to
Bellaghy one of our County's greatest sons.
The closing words uttered and beautifully sung by a successor
of Saint Patrick, in his adored Latin language,
were those of that hymn so popular in the time of his childhood
- Salve Regina.
The assembled followers, of the most humble of Irish poetic
icons, gently applauded.
Seamus was back in the place that he never really left.
Welcome home my old mentor. Noli timere.

(36) Albert Reynolds
– The Courageous Peacebroker

The young Albert Reynolds quickly learned the two most
important characteristics of any businessman.
The first was to have perceptive, all-inclusive, negotiating skills.
The other was to be always prepared to take a risk, especially if
the eventual reward was worth fighting for.
In the early 1960's, a personal, life-changing experience had
endorsed these basic ground rules.
One night, the Roscommon show business impresario was
listening to Radio Luxembourg.
He was so enamoured with the brilliant musicianship of a new
English trumpeter, called Kenny Ball
That he immediately booked him, six months in advance, for a
ten-night tour of Ireland.
Incredibly, by the time the gig came around, the previously
unknown artist was
On top of the international hit parade with his now legendary
rendition of" Midnight in Moscow."
Lucky Albert had made such a "financial killing" that he bought
his Longford family home with the tour's profits!

Thirty years later, on his first day as Taoiseach, he stood on the
podium
And announced that a peaceful resolution of the seemingly
insoluble Northern Ireland conflict
Was the number one priority on his political agenda.

Within weeks Reynolds, "the doer", had convinced his long-
standing friend, English Prime Minister, John Major, to do
likewise.
Simultaneously, he also opened exploratory talks
With the four different stakeholders of the Northern
community
While, at the same time, initiating private meetings with
representatives of the loyalist paramilitaries.
The cumulative result of all these wide-ranging deliberations
was
That both sovereign governments were eventually in a position
to plan a specific strategy for the future.
This they officially, unequivocally, expressed in their joint
Downing Street Declaration in December, 1993.

It stated that only the whole people of Ireland would have the
right to their self-determination.
And that the people of Northern Ireland could not be forced,
against their will, to join a United Ireland.
It also pledged to hold settlement negotiations with every party,
including Sinn Féin,
Provided they and their paramilitary ally - the IRA - would
agree to a permanent cessation of violence.
Reynolds was now seen at his most persuasive, his diplomatic
best, when he convinced President Bill Clinton
To grant American visas to Sinn Féin's Gerry Adams and
former IRA chief of staff, Joe Cahill.
This was their price for agreeing to the IRA ceasefire that
commenced in August, 1994.
Six weeks later, the loyalist paramilitaries laid down their arms.

All Ireland rejoiced - euphoria swept the streets of Derry and
Belfast.
A longed - for peace was now a definite prospect.

In essence, this declaration was the fundamental framework
On which the Good Friday Agreement in 1998 was based.
For twenty-five years John Hume had been the most vociferous,
the hardest-working advocate for a peaceful outcome.
Many other Taoisigh, British Prime Ministers, American
Presidents, Northern politicians, community activists, had
played pivotal roles.
But, from a Southern perspective, Albert Reynolds was the
person that took the greatest risks.
The determined, courageous Taoiseach once travelled alone
into the heartland of loyalist Belfast,
Just to assure their leaders that they too could join peace talks if
they called off their campaign of violence.
In the 1960's, Albert had used two distinct principles to
progress his personal business ambitions.
Now, in the 1990's, he utilised the same, defining criteria,
regardless of his personal safety,
To ensure a peaceful reconciliation of an age-old problem for all
of the people of Ireland.

(37) Keeper Of The Faith

After centuries of religious persecution came emancipation
And a welcome opportunity for the previously disenfranchised,
To fully celebrate their inherent,Catholic faith.
New, structurally sound churches and schools were planned
and promptly established,
As a necessary expression of people's innate, deeply held
beliefs,
As bastions for securing what was conscientiously handed
down,
For several generations by their forefathers,
In difficult, social circumstances, at much personal sacrifice for
many.

From the seven counties in our diocese,
They travelled, in unprecedented numbers, with their shillings,
their pennies
And an all-embracing, fulsome generosity of spirit to make me
what I am;
Externally, a building of splendid church architecture:
internally, a magnificently ornate edifice,
A fitting tribute to the wonder of God on a Longford skyline,
But, more importantly, a complete personification
Of an intrinsic, intimate spirituality,
An integral part of the faithful's minds, their hearts, their past.

Forty thousand people attended the laying of my foundation stone.

In those pre-famine times, all of them walked barefooted: some a return journey of over sixty miles.

They came to honour God in a powerful, public manifestation of his universality, his unique importance to them.

Despite the enormous constraints imposed by famine, disease, poverty, meagre incomes,

The diocese's parishioners continued to manually support the evolving construction process: to donate their precious pennies,

Until the whole mammoth project was finished, over fifty years later.

Materially, they may have been poor but, in essence, they were extremely rich in what mattered most,

The moral values of faith, trust, support, loyalty.

I have been the focal point, the catalyst

For thousands of children as they made their first faith journey,

Up the aisle, to be inducted into Christianity.

And for over a hundred and fifty years I have been an ever – present conduit

For the daily enactment of the Eucharist;

The joyful occasions of First Communion, Confirmation, Matrimony and Ordination.

It has been my privilege to facilitate the support, the consoling of the bereaved,

During their loved ones last earthly pathway: their final commendation from this life to the next.

Thanks to a multiplicity of beautiful choirs, soloists, talented organists,

Liturgical music in all its varied genres,

Has regularly graced my inner sanctum, my inner walls.

No finer musical rendition was there than that of a Christmas Eve

On which an unassuming successor of St Mel gave a particularly, moving and, consequently, most apt homily.

Little did I then realise that only a few hours later,

An accidental fire would utterly engulf and totally destroy my whole interior

And leave, in the short term, a town, a county, a diocese,

without its living spiritual home, its magnetic epicentre.

Just as the people worked, prayed and saved for my first coming,

I have no doubt that those entrusted to restoring my physical beauty

To its former glory, will do likewise for my second.

As St Mel's Cathedral, I look forward once again

To being the fulcrum, the spiritual core

Of the See of Ardagh and Clonmacnois.

I cannot wait until that Great Tomorrow comes

And I will once more be united with and etched, indelibly,

in the minds, hearts and memories of a renewed, revitalised people.

(38) The Pride Of Kilbride

People involved in organised armed conflict
Against those who governed them,
Or personnel, who fought with any sector of their own
countries' defence forces,
Against a foreign oppressor and died in the process,
Were perceived, traditionally, as the only, definitive type of
patriot.
As we have become more civilised, more egalitarian,
There is a greater awareness, an increasing authenticity,
That those who spill sweat, not blood,
To ensure that others have a better quality of life and a safer,
happier existence,
Are the real patriots, the unsung and unseen heroes of our
society, our times.

No one epitomised that kind of self-sacrifice, that fearless
generosity of spirit,
More than twenty four year old Garda Ciarán Jones of Manor
Kilbride.
One late, Autumn evening in 2011, the whole of Dublin and
surrounding counties
Were subjected to a torrential monsoon of incessant rain, an
unparalleled downpour of epic proportions.
As he was walking, near his home, the swell of the nearby River
Liffey
Rose rapidly, almost to bursting point, near Ballysmuttan
Bridge.
But, even though he was off duty, the worried and considerate

Garda redirected many motorists away from the bridge,
In case it would collapse and cause a major catastrophe.
Unfortunately, the raging, flash floods suddenly enveloped his
whole body
And swept him, mercilessly, into the gushing, gathering waters
of the river and onto his premature, tragic death.

So, the young football captain who had led his club to a county
title
And proudly wore the Senior jersey, of his native Wicklow, was
no more.
His courageous act of gallantry, in the fleeting moments of
unexpected adversity,
Had quenched the flame of a promising career, a happy, family
life.
For his parents, brother, sister and his beloved Clare, the loss
was the greatest, the most difficult to comprehend.
Clare's words of positivity at his funeral Mass offered real hope
for the future.
"Our hearts are broken but I have no doubt
He will continue to protect us - Ciarán was and is the pride of
Kilbride."
An ordinary man who did an extraordinary good turn so that
others could live.
Ciarán Jones will be forever respected and remembered - a real
Guardian of the Peace - a real Irish patriot.

(39) Ardagh Of Saint Mel

A place of architectural beauty, inherent splendour;
"Inseparately connected, inextricably woven into the whole tapestry
Of the faith and history of the diocese;"
Steeped in the totality of the past, the creation of the present;
The jewel in Longford's contribution to the spread of Christianity.
The ancient cyclopean limestone ruins of an eighth century church,
The classical cast-iron railings on the peripheries and a rare lych churchyard gate
Are but some of the charming artefacts
Which reflect its wonderfully, enchanted heritage,
Its current picturesque landscape impressively flanked by the marvellously designed Church of St Brigid.

After Patrick lit the first paschal fire on the Hill of Slane,
He and his followers moved westwards across a countryside interspersed with fort settlements, earthen raths.
In these embryonic habitats, hundreds were converted to the Christian faith,
Before they crossed the River Inny into the modern county of Longford.
At Ardagh he got permission from Maine, the local, pagan chieftain and brother of the High King, Laoghaire,
To evangelise the people under his jurisdiction.
A wooden church was built; a loyal follower called Mel was appointed bishop.

And Patrick, the missionary, then travelled onto other places, other people.

But the community that he left behind, rapidly developed into a Christian fortress.

And for over a thousand years it was the spiritual headquarters, the epicentre of a whole diocese.

Ardagh provided literary inspiration for Oliver Goldsmith

In his widely-acclaimed, comedy play, "She Stoops to Conquer"

The Fetherson family, proprietors of the magnificent and adjacent Ardagh demesne, in the nineteenth century,

Decided to remodel the developing village into a planned estate,

Of Swiss-styled latticed windows with cut stone surrounds, gabled doorways, ornate chimneys,

Arranged around a central village green whose dominant feature was an imposing, Gothic clock tower.

The result of all this meticulous planning, this aesthetically, intrinsic elegance,

Was to see Ardagh thrice crowned as the tidiest village in Ireland.

Subsequently, it has become a majestic presence for historians, architects and tourists alike.

What a fitting tribute to its founding father, its patron saint, its very own Saint Mel.

(40) From Ardoyne To Arás An Uachtaráin

True greatness only manifests itself
When the individual bestowed with such a gift can actually
"Walk with kings without losing the common touch."
So it is with Mary McAleese, barrister, academic, and
journalist.
But, more importantly, a People's President in the "bits and
pieces" of everyday life.
From the youngest child to the oldest adult, she has empathised
In their joys, sorrows, challenges and dreams.
Making them all feel wanted, influential in what they did or said.

Twenty-five years before her inauguration, the dark side of the
Troubles
Forced her and her family from their home to a safer place.
It had been one of the worst years of the Northern conflict
as a sequence of intimidation, sectarianism, shootings, and
bombings engulfed her native city.
She, like many others, had experienced the death of family
friends, the ongoing threat of sectarian violence in a raw, Belfast
interface.
On December 8th, two gunmen stepped from their car outside
the McAleese homestead,
Took out two machine guns, riddled the house with numerous
bullets.
Luckily the whole family were at Mass.
Otherwise the course of Irish history could have been tragically
altered.

Undeterred, she courageously looked ahead; studied diligently,
performed brilliantly in a number of challenging roles.
By 1997 the bright, young girl from Ardoyne had assumed the
highest office in the land.
For the next fourteen years she undertook her state and
ambassadorial duties
With absolute dedication, dignity, aplomb.
Her presidential theme of building bridges was carefully,
sensitively, implemented
Amongst all sectors within the Republic, between North and
South, between Britain and Ireland.
With the mental strength, the diplomatic expertise of Martin,
her very supportive husband,
Excellent relations were created and delicately forged amongst
the Unionist and Loyalist traditions in Northern Ireland.

After she became President, initially,
She made her first official, overseas trip to South Lebanon,
To pay homage to the work done by the Irish peacekeeping
troops.
At that time, the physical signs of conflict there were very much
in evidence.
And back at home, the Good Friday Agreement was but a pipe
dream.
In October 2011, she returned, to both jurisdictions, for the last
time as President.
Now, in each region, the impact of peace was clearly to be seen.
In the interim she had visited many other countries where she
always presented a positive view of Ireland, thus helping to
attract foreign investment and tourism back home.

For the first time, in a century, an English monarch
Came to Ireland, for an official visit, in May, 2011.
Among the venues Queen Elizabeth visited were the Garden of
Remembrance and Croke Park:
Both very much associated with Ireland's ancient, bitter quarrel
with England.
For her and us this was a great, symbolic gesture in the mutual
normalisation of harmonious relations.
No one did more to prepare, crystallise this wonderful
development
Than Mary Patricia McAleese, President of Ireland, 1997-
2011.
Amongst a variety of fantastic achievements this was,
undoubtedly, her finest legacy to her native country.

Bibliography

I would like to gratefully acknowledge the following publications and individuals for providing me with important, background material in the compilation of this book.

Ardagh and Clonmacnois - Footprints of Mel and Ciaran. Very Rev Canon Owen Devaney P.P. Mullahoran, Co. Cavan.

Ballinascreen Historical Society, Draperstown, Co. Derry. (per Graham Mawhinney and Patsy McShane).

Harry's Game by Harry Gregg (Mainstream Publishing).

The Road to Bloody Sunday by the late Dr Raymond McClean (Guildhall Press).

Stanley Matchett Photography for their kind permission in allowing use of their iconic Bloody Sunday photograph on front cover.

Thank You

A special thank you to Joe Hunt of Legan, Co. Longford, for the highly efficient manner, as always, in which he undertook the meticulous task of proofing.